BASICS OF
CHRISTIAN
EDUCATION

BASICS OF
CHRISTIAN
EDUCATION

KAREN B. TYE

Chalice Press.
St. Louis, Missouri

Bible quotations, unless otherwise noted, are from the *New Revised Standard Version Bible*, copyright 1989, Division of Christian Education of the National Council of the Churches of Christ in the United States of America. Used by permission. All rights reserved.

Those quotations marked RSV are from the *Revised Standard Version of the Bible*, copyright 1952, [2nd edition, 1971] by the Division of Christian Education of the National Council of the Churches of Christ in the United States of America. Used by permission. All rights reserved.

Cover photography: © by PhotoDisc
Cover design: Elizabeth Wright
Art direction: Elizabeth Wright
Interior design: Wynn Younker

This book is printed on acid-free, recycled paper.

Visit Chalice Press on the World Wide Web at
www.chalicepress.com

10 9 8 7 6 5 4 3 2 1   00 01 02 03 04 05

Library of Congress Cataloging–in–Publication Data

Tye, Karen.
  Basics of Christian education / Karen Tye.
    p.   cm.
  ISBN 0-8272-0229-6
  1. Christian Education.   I. Title.
BV 1471.2 .T94 2000
268 – dc21   00-008132

Printed in the United States of America

In memory of my mother,
Roberta Bartmess Tye,
who taught me to love the church;
and
for my students
—past, present, and future—
who give me hope for its tomorrow.

CONTENTS

ACKNOWLEDGMENTS

This work has been several years in the making. Its roots, in fact, stretch far beyond the moment when the first words were put on the page. The seeds were planted long ago and nourished by my childhood community of faith, First Christian Church of Richmond, Indiana. I am grateful to the teachers and members of that community who nurtured my love and passion for the church.

The seeds were nourished in adulthood by many who provided support and encouragement. I am particularly grateful to my friend and former pastor, Steve Jones, without whose challenging words I might never have answered my call to teach, and to my mentors in my doctoral work—Dr. Charles Melchert, Dr. Ronald Cram, and Dr. Sara Little—who broadened my vision and modeled for me the importance of critical thinking for the educational ministry of the church. I also want to express my thanks to those who have read and commented on drafts of this work, especially Bob Fulbright, Kim Coffing, and my good friend and colleague from Australia, Dr. Christine Gapes. A word of thanks is due my faculty colleagues, the administration, and the board of directors of Eden Theological Seminary for their willingness to grant the sabbatical time that facilitated my writing efforts.

Finally, two groups receive my deepest and heartfelt gratitude. First, my husband, Brent Dodge, and my children, David and Kathy Brock, whose continuing support and belief in me have been a sustaining presence throughout the twists and turns of this journey. And last, my students, past and present, who have been my research colleagues as they have engaged the ideas presented in this book and have provided helpful and encouraging reflections as the work evolved. I couldn't have done it without you!

INTRODUCTION

The phone rang. It was a pastor calling to ask a favor. In the course of the conversation, as so often happened with these calls, we found ourselves talking about the educational ministry of his church. We shared a mutual interest in, and commitment to, this important ministry.

He voiced his ongoing concern about what was and was not happening in Christian education with his congregation. He knew that Christian education was vital to the life of the community of faith. Yet the traditional approaches did not seem to be working. Sunday school attendance was down, the lack of participation by the youth of the church was a continuing problem, and it was an ongoing struggle to find church school teachers and youth group sponsors. Any attempts at adult education drew a meager response. He wondered aloud, "What can we do?"

This was not a new conversation for me. I have shared in many such conversations in the course of my work as a seminary professor of Christian education. And I hear this conversation taking place in the wider church, given impetus by the results of the major study on effective Christian education conducted by Search Institute and first published in the spring of 1990. This study highlighted problems related to Christian education in several of the mainline Protestant churches and raised many of the same issues and concerns voiced by my pastor friend.

Called "Effective Christian Education: A National Study of Protestant Congregations,"[1] the study grew out of the concern of Protestant Christian education staffs at both the denominational and local levels about the health of Christian education. These concerns involved several areas. Prominent among them were (1) a disinterest among adults in adult

1

educational programs, (2) the failure of congregations to maintain involvement of their youth after the eighth grade, (3) the increasing difficulty in finding and keeping volunteer teachers, (4) the apparent lack of interest of clergy in education, (5) a problem in drawing parents into the educational process, and (6) the apparent failure of current programs and educational methods to address adequately and appropriately the changing needs and interest of adults, adolescents, and children.[2]

Needing information with which to analyze and address their concerns, six major Protestant denominations,[3] representing about 85 percent of the membership in what is called "mainline Protestantism," launched a national three-and-a-half-year study of Christian education. What they discovered was sobering. Their findings included:

> Only a minority of Protestant adults evidence the kind of integrated, vibrant, and life-encompassing faith that congregations seek to develop. For most adults, faith is underdeveloped, lacking some of the key elements necessary for faith maturity.

> A majority of adolescents fall into the faith type called "undeveloped faith."

> Only about three out of ten high school students (grades 10–12) and adults in mainline Protestant denominations are actively involved in Christian education.[4]

Researchers concluded that:

> Christian education in a majority of congregations is a tired enterprise in need of reform. Often out-of-touch with adult and adolescent needs, it experiences increasing difficulty in finding and motivating volunteers, faces general disinterest among its "clients," and employs models and procedures that have changed little over time.[5]

A critically important finding of the research was that Christian education mattered! It mattered even more than had been expected, especially in terms of a person's growth in faith and ability to be an active part of the community of faith. Researchers found a strong relationship between growth in faith maturity and active participation in a quality Christian education program. More than any other factor in congregational life, Christian education was key in the development of faith maturity and active church involvement. The research report concluded:

> In summary, Christian education matters. We see its power in the area of both life biographies and current congregational life. And we see it in both faith maturity and loyalty. The practical implication is clear: If a congregation seeks to strengthen its impact on faith and loyalty, involving members of all ages in quality Christian education is essential.[6]

It went on to say, "Effective Christian education has the potential, as much or more than any other congregational influence, to deepen faith, commitment, and loyalty. Its revitalization must therefore move to center stage."[7]

To me it seems important for the vitality and future of the church that we take seriously these issues and findings of the national study and that we give ear to the concerns it raised and to those expressed by my pastor friend. For the sake of the future of the church we must give our attention to Christian education and move this important ministry to center stage. It is important that we find ways in which to renew and transform this vital ministry of the church.

However, we also need to hear a word of caution. In our desire to respond to the findings of the Search Institute study and to address my pastor friend's question, "What do we do?" we need to be careful that we are not seduced by the "quick fix," grasping for the latest technique, technology, or newest prepackaged program that suggests to the church that uses it that it will then have a successful educational ministry (success here is usually defined and measured in terms of numbers).

Hopefully, our desire in addressing the question, What do we do? about Christian education is not to "create a nation of McChurches with bland, prepackaged programs and innocuous decor."[8] Instead, our purpose should be engagement in the kind of serious, creative, and intentional reflection, analysis, assessment, and planning that will enable us to renew and transform our understanding and practice of Christian education.

So where do we begin? What could my pastor friend "do" in response to his concerns? One of the responses that has emerged in the wider debate in our country about public education is captured by the slogan "Back to basics." Although I believe there is a danger in thinking that the way we did things and understood them in the past is the solution to present-day concerns, there is truth in the call to look at the "basics," at what is central and necessary for education. Too often in the church we have not talked about the basics. Instead, we have assumed that we know what we are doing and why we are doing it, and we've looked for "quick fixes" for anything that went wrong. I see this reflected in the students who arrive in my seminary classes. They often assume that they know what Christian education is all about, and they are merely looking for some new methods, techniques, curriculum resources, or *the* current program that will solve the Christian education problems in the churches they serve. But they have seldom thought about the basics.

Let me give an illustration. I am an amateur quilter. I have been sewing since I was a child, but I became interested in quilting about a decade ago. At first I thought quilting was as easy as sewing a seam together. I would look at the quilts on display at a quilt show and think, *I could do that!* But my first attempts at quilting never looked quite like those I saw on display. Then I took my first quilting class and was introduced to the basics. It was a whole new world. I learned about fabric and its selection, about piecing and constructing a quality block, about assembling the parts of a quilt, and about the quilting process itself. All these are basic to making a quilt. Even though the quilts that are created look very different from one another, the basics that one needs to know and understand remain the same.

I believe the same is true with educational ministry in the church. Although each church, given its own unique context and people, will have a Christian education program that is particular to that gathered community of faith, the basic concepts and building blocks necessary for developing a dynamic and nurturing Christian education ministry are the same. I believe it is vitally important at this point in the church's life that we take the time to consider these basics. We need to look at the foundational pieces by which a Christian education ministry is built. When we have an understanding of these pieces, we are then able to plan and build an educational ministry appropriate to the needs and concerns of a particular community of faith.

Another illustration I use with my students is that of a doctor and a patient. When a patient comes to a doctor wanting to know what he can do to feel better, the doctor does not begin with telling the patient what to do, drawing on the latest fad or technique in the medical world. Instead, she does a careful examination of the patient and what is basic to him—his symptoms, his lifestyle, and his family history. Only after this descriptive process is complete does the physician offer a plan of treatment, a prescription based on a basic knowledge of the patient himself.

Too often in the church we begin with "prescribing a course of treatment," choosing to use the latest denominational program or the newest curriculum resources, before we have given careful attention to the basics of educational ministry: what it is, why we do it, and so on. Only after we have done this basic work will we know what we need to do, what we need to "prescribe" for our particular educational ministry.

What are these basic building blocks for educational ministry? I believe at least six basic areas should be given attention when we are planning for and building an educational program in the church. These six foundational areas are (1) concept, (2) purpose, (3) context, (4) content, (5) participants, and (6) process and method. Each of these basic building blocks calls us to ask key questions. For CONCEPT, the main question is, What *is* Christian education? How do we define this term? What does it mean to call something *education*? And what does it mean to say that it is *Christian* education? PURPOSE asks, What is the purpose of Christian education? Why do we do it? What do we hope to have happen? For CONTEXT, the question is, Where does Christian education occur? What kinds of settings and environments are important? CONTENT draws our attention to what is taught, studied, and learned. What kinds of knowledge do Christians need to have? What will we teach? PARTICIPANTS leads us to the question, Who are the participants in this ministry? What do we need to know and understand about them? And finally, PROCESS AND METHOD raises the question, How do we do it? How will this education be done? What process and methods are appropriate to use, and how will we choose them?

In the following chapters, each of these basic building blocks will be discussed, and we will look at the issues and concerns the questions posed raise for us. At the end of each chapter, questions and exercises are offered to help readers use the particular building block in the planning and developing of educational ministry in their own unique settings. In addition to the six building blocks of educational ministry, I look at two other issues of importance to the vitality of our educational ministries. The first is the issue of ASSESSMENT AND EVALUATION. We need to have ways in which we look at what we are doing and assess how it is working. Too often in the church we undertake a program, it doesn't work in the ways we had hoped, and it is abandoned without any effort to find out what really happened. This can lead to waste and a constant "reinventing of the wheel" syndrome that does not reflect good stewardship on the part of the church. Learning to assess and evaluate is an important part of a vital educational ministry. The second issue I have named HINDRANCES. We need to look at the kinds of resistance we will face, both in ourselves and in our congregations, when we commit ourselves to renewing and revitalizing our educational ministries. However deep our passion, there is still that within us, both as individuals and as communities of faith, that resists change. Understanding this can help us keep resistance from blocking our efforts.

I am aware that you may not hear much that seems new to you in the pages that follow. You may think on occasion, *Of course, I knew that.* As I said at the beginning, this is about the basics and recalling to our attention what is foundational to the educational ministry of the church. My hope is that the pastors, Christian educators, seminary students, concerned laity, and others who read this work will be renewed in their commitment to this vital ministry and will build on the basics to renew and transform Christian education for the sake of the church and its mission in the world.

Chapter 1

CONCEPT:
What Is Christian Education?

It happens each time. Everything is quiet as they sit with somewhat puzzled looks on their faces. It is the first day of class, and I have just asked the students in the seminary's required course on the foundations of Christian education to respond in writing to the question, What is Christian education? After a few moments, there is a rustle of papers as students begin to write, many of them still with a little frown wrinkling their foreheads.

As we talk afterward, I find out that this is the first time many of them have thought about this question. In fact, it is the first time many of them have had the question asked of them. They have heard the term *Christian education* used often, but they've never stopped to think about what it means. They simply assumed that they knew, that everyone else in the church also knew, and that they were all in agreement.

This same phenomenon happens with regularity when I work with a local church's Christian education committee. When I ask them to respond to the question, What is Christian education? one of two things generally occurs. Either committee members seem puzzled and, after some reflection, indicate that they have never really thought about it before, or they begin talking about Sunday school and teaching children. Their primary points of reference for Christian education are children and Sunday school. Although I would not argue that Christian education involves Sunday school and children, to define it in these terms is limiting and does not provide an adequate foundation on which to build this important ministry.

Why is our CONCEPT of Christian education a basic building block for educational ministry? Why is it important to ask the question, What is Christian education? I believe it is important because it will determine what we do in the name of Christian education. Our understanding of what it is will influence and shape what we do, why we do it, and how we go about this vital ministry of the church. As one of my mentors, Dr. Charles Melchert, once said,

> If we are unclear about what it is or what we are looking for in the process, the best we can hope for is to get where we are going part of the time by accident. I would suggest both our people and our God are entitled to expect more of us than that.[1]

Like Melchert, I believe we should not be carrying out the church's educational ministry by accident or happenstance. We need to have some clarity about what we are doing. It is too important a ministry not to have thought through what it means in order to then give it our best efforts.

When I look at the life and ministry of Jesus, I am struck by how important it was that he named clearly who he was and what he was about. The story of his temptation seems to me to be a story of his coming to clarity about his own identity, of his being able to name both what it meant and what it did not mean to be called the Son of God. It seems significant that Luke's telling of the temptation story (Lk. 4:1–13) is followed by a description of Jesus' visit to the synagogue in Nazareth where he boldly names the ministry to which he is called (Lk. 4:14–21). In this naming, he places before himself and his listeners a clear picture of the path he will follow. And the gospels bear evidence that he was true to his name and to the claims of his ministry.

However, I want to speak a word of caution here. I do not think that the goal of working with the building block of concept is to come up with one common definition, a kind of "one-size-fits-all" approach. Like the noted Christian educator Thomas Groome, I believe that the enterprise of education is too complex for there to be one universally agreed upon definition.[2] Instead, my goal is for the church to have an open and honest conversation about what Christian education is, what we think we are doing. Through such a conversation we can name those assumptions we take for granted, we can talk about the concept of Christian education that seems to be implicitly at work in our congregation, and we can look at ways in which our taken-for-granted definition may be limiting or preventing us from carrying out a more effective educational ministry.

Ways of Defining Christian Education

What are some ways in which we might define Christian education? How might we give some shape and form to this building block? When working with the issue of concept with students or local congregations, I often begin by asking them to tell what Christian education already means to them. The list of words and phrases has grown considerably over the years. Those I have heard repeated time and again include:

nurture	conversion
instruction	habit formation
teaching	indoctrination
development	catechesis
critical thinking	socialization
transmitting the faith	character formation
growth	moral development
conserving the faith	transformation
faith development	schooling
spiritual formation	belief formation

It seems to be quite a varied list, and the words don't all appear to suggest the same thing. However, I think there is a way to make some sense out of this rather diverse list and begin to distinguish some core characteristics of Christian education.

As I studied these responses over time, they suggested to me four ways of understanding Christian education.[3] The first sees Christian education as *religious instruction*. The terms *teaching, instruction, transmitting the faith, conserving the faith, indoctrination, catechesis, belief formation,* and *schooling* suggest this understanding.

This definition of Christian education highlights deliberate and intentional efforts by the church to transmit the knowledge and practices of the Christian faith. Although I agree with Sara Little that we must be careful not to equate instruction with the school setting,[4] this definition does focus on the more formal and structured teaching process for the passing on of knowledge, especially facts and information, and the acquisition of certain beliefs.

The second definition of Christian education that emerges from our list of terms is that of a *socialization process.* Jack Seymour and Donald Miller call this the faith community approach.[5] Others have called it the "community of faith enculturation" model.[6] Terms like *nurture, socialization, habit formation, enculturation,* and even *conversion,* depending on how one understands this process,[7] point to this definition.

To define Christian education in this manner highlights the ways in which people become a part of a particular group, take on its identity, and acquire its beliefs, habits, and behaviors. It calls attention to how people come to know who they are and what they believe through their interactions with those in the church. Such an understanding of Christian education would certainly value participation in the worship services—hearing the hymns, prayers, and spoken word and taking part in the various ritual acts, such as communion—as an important way in which children and youth learn what it means to be a Christian. As Charles Foster says, "We know we are Christian because we participate in Christianity's historical embodiment (i.e., the church)."[8]

The third way of defining Christian education that I see reflected in the list is the *personal development approach.* The words *growth, faith development, spiritual formation, moral development,* and *character formation* are suggestive of this approach.

This understanding of Christian education finds its roots in developmental theory, which suggests that there is a structure of growth involving various steps or stages through which every individual moves and that education is a process that assists this growth. Defining Christian education as personal development highlights the need for an environment that nurtures all persons in whatever stage they are in on their faith journey and helps them move from stage to stage. The reliance on age-graded curriculum resources in the church school is one indication of the presence of this approach. The key characteristic to remember here is the emphasis on nurturing and assisting individuals in growing and maturing through their own personal spiritual journeys. Education is understood primarily as an individual rather than a communal activity.

The remaining definition of Christian education that I see reflected in the list of terms is a *process of liberation.* The terms *critical thinking* and *transformation* point to this approach. Education as liberation is concerned with transformation, the "forming over" of the church, of persons, and of society. Such education emphasizes the "development of a new Christian consciousness which will be aware of the global context of oppression and will lead Christians in constructing new, faithful, lifestyles."[9]

Seen in this way, education becomes a prophetic activity. It seeks to develop critical reflection skills and enable participation in social action. This concept of Christian education calls for direct involvement in the world through activities such as mission trips and community service projects rather than remaining in traditional church contexts such as church school.

My own experience tells me that these four definitions of Christian education—as religious instruction, as socialization, as personal development, and as liberation—are present in the church, shaping what we do as educational ministry. Although I believe that these are not the only concepts of Christian education at work in the church today, I do think that these are representative of the more prevalent viewpoints. I also believe that these seldom exist in "pure form." You may have been thinking as you read each of the descriptions that some aspect of each description would fit your setting. The church with which you are familiar may emphasize the church school and formal religious instruction. Yet it also uses age-graded curriculum resources. And it encourages participation by children in the worship service so that they can come to know the appropriate responses and behaviors for members of that faith community.

My purpose for naming these various definitions is not to create a set of mutually exclusive concepts from which we are to choose the "correct" one. Instead, I see these various descriptions offering us an opportunity to reflect on and think about how each of us would name Christian education in our own church setting. Are there ways in which we limit ourselves because we have defined education from only one perspective? Are there ways in which we need to expand our definitions in order to carry out more vital educational ministries? This important building block is the key to such vitality.

Laying the Foundation: Developing a Definition

Although each of these meanings of Christian education is present in the church, I believe that any given congregation tends to emphasize one over the others. Much of this is rooted in habit–we've always done it this way–and the fact that we do not often talk about such basic things as our concepts of Christian education. We tend to emphasize a certain approach, and it becomes the primary vision that shapes our educational ministry. Many churches emphasize formal religious instruction as the primary meaning of Christian education and put their energies into formal church school programs and Bible studies. Other churches give emphasis to the personal development approach and build their education programs around small sharing groups that provide nurturing environments for exploring one's life journey and discerning God's presence and leading. Still others take a strong liberation approach and focus energy on mission and service as the means by which one truly learns about the life of discipleship.

The difficulty comes when we operate out of one narrow definition of Christian education and are unable to see other ways of understanding what we are doing. Daniel Aleshire points out, "One purpose of a definition is to erect a fence to distinguish what is inside from what is outside."[10] However, he goes on to argue, the fence can be too small and leave too many things outside. He calls for a broad definition of Christian education. As he puts it, "A broad definition does not require us to change what is done at church so much as it causes us to look at it differently."[11] Given the shifting sands of the times in which we live, there is strong evidence of the need for the four approaches to educational ministry mentioned, and I believe our task in the church is to work at integrating these perspectives into our own definitions of Christian education.

Aleshire offers a definition that is suggestive of how we might integrate various approaches into a broader vision. He defines Christian education this way:

Christian education involves those tasks and expressions of ministry that enable people (1) to learn the Christian story, both ancient and present; (2) to develop the skills they need to act out their faith; (3) to reflect on that story in order to live self-aware to its truth; and (4) to nurture the sensitivities they need to live together as a covenant community.[12]

I believe he is certainly getting at the basics of Christian education and, in doing so, integrates the various approaches named above. "To learn the Christian story" suggests an instructional process that provides people with the information and facts that they need about this story. "To develop the skills they need to act out their faith" suggests a focus on action in the world and points to a liberation process. "To reflect on that story in order to live self-aware" calls for a personal development approach with an emphasis on growing and maturing in knowledge of self and one's individual faith journey. "To nurture the sensitivities...to live...as a community" suggests a socialization process with its emphasis on participation in the community of faith as a way in which to learn what it means to be Christian.

In presenting Aleshire's definition, I am not proposing that you adopt it as your own. Each congregation, working together, needs to do the work of defining education for itself. Instead, I offer it as an example of the kind of broad vision that I believe is needed in order to engage in effective educational ministry in the years to come.

I do not believe that a broad definition of Christian education is the result of sloppy thinking. I believe that a broad definition helps us to see the basics that are necessary in developing a strong and vital educational ministry. Education in the church calls for religious instruction, socialization, personal development, and liberation. There is a need for transmitting knowledge, for shaping people through their participation in their community's activities, for helping people on their individual faith journeys, and for developing a critical consciousness that leads to faithful service in the world.

Nor do I think that a special emphasis on a particular aspect of this broad definition means the absence of the other approaches. Even as my husband and I emphasize a certain color in the decorating scheme of our home, the presence of accent colors enlivens and enriches our living space. Even though a church may emphasize religious instruction in its educational ministry, the presence of an intentional socialization process, of efforts to nurture personal spiritual development, and of activities involving people in liberating service in the world can add vitality to that church's educational ministry and increase its effectiveness.

Broadening the Foundation

As you begin work on your own definition of Christian education, I believe that there are some other aspects of this foundational building block you need to consider. To do this, it is helpful to turn to another definition of Christian education, this one provided by noted educator Thomas Groome. He defines Christian education as:

> a political activity with pilgrims in time that deliberately and intentionally attends with them to the activity of God in our present, to the Story of the Christian faith community, and to the Vision of God's Kingdom, the seeds of which are already among us.[13]

There are three terms Groome uses in his definition that I believe are important to consider as we do our work of defining. Those words are *political, deliberately,* and *intentionally.* *Planning*

When my students first read this definition, they often express a strong resistance to the term *political.* It is almost a dirty word in our society. We equate political with the kind of partisan battles we see taking place daily in our governmental structures. At its root, however, the word comes from the Greek word *polis,* which means city, and refers to our social interactions as citizens. In using the term, Groome is highlighting the *social nature* of education.

Groome calls our attention to the communal and social nature of Christian education. What he helps us consider is how our education helps people to live in community, to participate in the wider society, and to live out their faith in and on behalf of the world. What he helps us remember is that Christian education is not an individual activity. It may be personal in that it is concerned with persons and their personal faith journeys. However, at its heart Christian education is a communal activity done by the community of faith on behalf of the community of faith for the benefit of, and for service to, the world. As we give thought to the definition of Christian education for our particular congregations, it is important that we remember the political nature of our work.

With the words *deliberately* and *intentionally*, Groome raises for us another important aspect of our educational work. To approach something deliberately means to give it careful thought. To be intentional about something means to plan for it to happen. The *Effective Christian Education* study discovered that planning was one of the vital elements in building and maintaining a strong educational ministry.[14] Yet it also discovered that many churches wander aimlessly, not knowing what they are doing or where they are going in Christian education.[15]

As I stated earlier, I believe Christian Education is too vital a ministry to let happen by accident or happenstance. We cannot wander from program to program and hope to prepare people for the life of discipleship in today's world. To be faithful to the mandate to go and teach (Mt. 28:20) requires our most intentional and deliberate efforts. However we come to define Christian education in the church, my hope is that we will faithfully carry out this ministry with deliberateness and intentionality.

There is a final aspect of this foundational building block of concept that I want to discuss. It has to do with the relationship of education and schooling. When I ask people to define Christian education for me, the most often used terms are *school* or *schooling*. For many people, Christian education is equated with school, specifically the church school.

I do not want to demean or diminish the role or place of the church school in educational ministry. I will say more about this in the chapter on context. However, I think we create problems for a broader and more vital vision of Christian education when we limit ourselves to the image of school. Maria Harris talks about this as "the false identification of education with only one of its forms: schooling."[16] As she points out,

> In this view, the participants in education are always "instructors" or "learners," the place of education is

necessarily a school (or a setting that replicates the school); the stuff of education is books and chalkboards and lesson plans; and the process involved is mental activity.[17]

Let us contrast this schooling image of education with an image we find in Deuteronomy 6:4–9. In this passage, Israel is given the heart of her religious teachings, the great commandment: "Hear, O Israel: The LORD is our God, the LORD alone. You shall love the LORD your God with all your heart, and with all your soul, and with all your might." This is followed with the way in which this teaching is to take place, with the presentation of what I would call an educational process. The Israelites are told:

> Keep these words that I am commanding you today in your heart. Recite them to your children and talk about them when you are at home and when you are away, when you lie down and when you rise. Bind them as a sign on your hand, fix them as an emblem on your forehead, and write them on the doorposts of your house and on your gates.

As we examine this text, we discover that education occurs in the context of the family, and that it is done in both formal (recite the words) and informal (talk about this at home, display signs and symbols that recall the teaching) ways. This seems to me to be in distinct contrast to the schooling model as described by Harris. Perhaps our Hebrew ancestors had a broader vision of education, a vision that is important for us to consider.

Connecting the activity of instruction only with school is limiting. If we identify instruction only with school and formal teaching settings, we overlook the fact that instruction can take place in a variety of settings other than school.

I think of my husband, Brent, and his young grandson, Phillip. Brent is a bread baker, and Phillip loves his grandpa's banana bread. Whenever they are together, Phillip wants Grandpa to make banana bread, and Phillip wants to help. So they gather together in the kitchen and Brent carefully and patiently guides Phillip through the process of making the bread. He is "instructing" him, although there are no signs of "school" around. In time Phillip will learn to make banana bread on his own. He will have been taught, "instructed" how to do it, but none of that experience will be thought of as "school."

Just as the kitchen becomes a place of instruction, so too does the church sanctuary or the fellowship hall or the church-sponsored soup kitchen or the family living room. We provide religious instruction in a variety of ways and a variety of settings. To understand Christian education as more than school and to see the possibilities of religious instruction beyond the schooling model offers us a broader and more vital perspective on this important ministry.

Summary

A definition of Christian education is a foundational building block in the educational ministry of the church. It is through our definitions that we become aware of the essential aspects of this important ministry and enable ourselves to be more effective at it. I trust that this discussion about the various perspectives on Christian education has stimulated the readers to give careful thought to both their own and their churches' definitions and to consider ways in which these definitions might be broadened to bring new energy and life.

Recall the finding of the *Effective Christian Education* study that Christian education matters, and it matters a great deal! Being clear on what it is that we are doing can only increase education's ability to make a difference in the life of our own church.

The word *education* comes from the Latin *educare*, meaning to lead out or to lead forth. At its heart, education is an activity of leading out or leading forth. If we hope to lead people forth into lives of faith and committed discipleship, we will need our clearest and best thinking and the most deliberate and intentional efforts we can muster. The church of Jesus Christ deserves no less!

Reflection and Application

The following exercises are offered to assist readers in their engagement with the ideas presented in this chapter.

1. Brainstorm your own list of synonyms for Christian education. Compare and contrast with the list presented in this chapter. What is the same? What is different? What do you think your list reflects about your understanding of Christian education?

2. Interview several church members (include people of all ages), asking them how they would define Christian education. Add their words to the above list. What do you think this list reflects about the wider church's understanding of Christian education?

3. Rank your list of terms. Which words or phrases come the closest to representing the definition of Christian education at work in your church? How would you describe this understanding of Christian education? Compare your definition with the four approaches to Christian education presented on pages 10–12. Is there a similarity with one of these approaches? Which one? Do you find the presence of any of the other approaches in your church? Which ones?

4. Write your own definition of Christian education. What is emphasized in your definition? What is not? Why?

5. How might you share this definition with the wider church? How might you invite its input? Prepare a plan of action for doing this.

Chapter 2

PURPOSE: *the aim + goal of our efforts.*
Why Do We Educate?

Tye: continuity + change

The time is approaching 10 p.m., and the Christian education committee has been meeting for more than two hours. You can see the fatigue in members' faces. There is a note of panic in the chairman's voice as he lists the details that still need to be settled. As he completes the list, Doris, who has been sitting quietly for most of the evening, suddenly speaks. You can hear the frustration in her voice. "I am so tired of these endless details and the constant surfacing of problems that need solution. We lurch from crisis to crisis, we plan event after event. And tonight it has suddenly hit me—Is it worth it? What is it that we are trying to do?"

Several of the members turn to her in surprise and begin speaking all at once. "Doris, I'm surprised at you. Surely you know why we are here." "I can't believe a good Christian lady like you would raise such a question!" Their responses tumble out, each with a reason for all his or her effort. Doris raises a hand to silence them and responds, "I think we are in the business of oiling machinery. And it doesn't matter if it is a necessary or useful machine just so long as it keeps running well, or running at all, for that matter. But what's it all for? What is our purpose?"[1]

Perhaps this scene is familiar. The long meetings and the attention to endless details are representative of all too many of the Christian education committee meetings in which I have participated. We may never have had the courage to voice Doris' question, but I have a hunch that we have thought about it. What are we trying to do? What's it all for? Why do we do Christian education?

This question is at the core of our second building block, PURPOSE. Purpose has to do with the aim and goal of our efforts. Just as it is important to define our concept of Christian education, it is equally important to know *why* we are doing it. If we are unclear as to why we are educating in the church, we can end up with outcomes that we did not intend. It is like taking a trip. If we do not know where we are going, for example New York City, then we could end up in Atlanta.

I believe that concept and purpose go hand in hand. We cannot fully engage in the various kinds of education, be it religious instruction, socialization, personal development, liberation, or whatever, unless we know the end toward which we are instructing, socializing, developing, and so on. Our purpose shapes what it is we do as education.

I think again of the example of Jesus. He was very clear as to the purpose of his ministry. Using the words of the prophet Isaiah, he claimed his goal of bringing good news to the poor, proclaiming release to the captives, recovery of sight to the blind, letting the oppressed go free, and proclaiming the year of the Lord's favor (Lk. 4:18–19). This core purpose of his ministry shaped what he did, where he went, what he said, and with whom he spent his time. His ministry was empowered by the clearness of his vision. A clarity of purpose will also provide shape to and empower our educational endeavors in the church.

What Are We Trying to Do?

What are some of the purposes of Christian education that we could name? Let's return to our Christian education committee meeting. When Doris expressed her frustration and asked the critical question, "What is it that we are trying to do?" several of the committee members responded with immediate answers. One said that the purpose of Christian education is to teach the Bible. Another said that it is to apply the Bible to life. A third committee member responded that it is to provide nurture and support for our personal faith journeys. A fourth person said that it is to transmit the Christian heritage to the next generation.[2]

All these seem like good answers. Teaching the Bible, learning to apply the Bible to life, providing nurture and support for people's spiritual journeys, and transmitting the faith heritage to the next generations are worthy purposes for our Christian education.

Daniel Aleshire's vision of Christian education, discussed in chapter 1, points to some similar purposes. He names four of them. First, Christian education is to enable people to learn the Christian story, both ancient and present. Second, it is to help people develop the skills they need to act out their faith, to live as Christians, as Christ's ones. Third, Christian education is to help people reflect on the Christian story so that they can live aware of the truth of the story and how that truth is present in their own lives. And finally, it is to nurture those sensitivities, attitudes, and abilities that people need to live and work together as a community of faith.[3]

Thomas Groome claims that the purpose of Christian education is "to enable people to live as Christians, that is, to live lives of Christian faith."[4] For him, this means to help people live their lives according to "God's own vision and intention for all people and creation," a vision that includes efforts on behalf of justice, human dignity, and freedom for all.[5]

It seems to me that all these purpose statements, those of the committee members and those of our authors, suggest some important goals for Christian education. We do want to transmit the Christian heritage to future generations. We do want to teach the Bible, learn to apply the Bible in our current life experiences, and develop skills for acting out our faith. We want to nurture and support each other on our faith journeys. We need to develop the skills and attitudes necessary to live as a community of faith and embody in our life together what it means to be Christian. We do want to teach what it means to live as though the realm of God is a reality, to live out a vision of justice and mercy, human dignity and worth, and freedom for all.

Is it possible, however, to look at these various purpose statements in a way that would integrate them into a broad vision of our purpose in Christian education? Is there a way to look at them as a whole and gain insight as to why we do

Christian education? I believe there is, and I want to propose a vision that might help us as we work to clarify the purpose of Christian education in our own congregational settings.

Continuity and Change

Walter Brueggemann says, "Every community that wants to last beyond a single generation must concern itself with education."[6] Education plays a vital role in the maintaining of a community through the generations. One of the purposes of education, then, is to ensure a "continuity of vision, value, and perception so that the community sustains its self-identity."[7] In other words, education has to do with continuity, with helping to carry forward across time the traditions and teachings that form the core and shape the life of a people.

However, Brueggemann also says that communities must be able to survive and be relevant and pertinent in new situations. For this to happen, education must be concerned with what he calls "discontinuity," or an emphasis on new ways of thinking. In other words, one of the purposes of education is to help things change, to help transform old traditions and teachings in order to bring new life to a people. For Brueggemann, "education must attend both to processes of continuity and discontinuity in order to avoid fossilizing into irrelevance on the one hand, and relativizing into disappearance on the other hand."[8]

Continuity and change. We all need roots, that which gives us a sense of connection, a sense of who we are, that is unbroken across time. I think that the strong interest in our society today in genealogy, in discovering our roots, is a sign of this need for connection. We want to know who we are, where we came from, and in whose footsteps we follow. This sense of continuity provides us with identity and gives some meaning and direction to our lives.

Yet we also know that change is a reality of life and is important for our growth and maturity. New situations and circumstances call on us to change, to take a different perspective, to transform an old way of doing something. I think of the story of the young bride who cut her ham in half before baking it. When her husband asked her why, she replied that it was because her mother always did it that way. The young bride asked her mother, and her mother said that that was the way her mother had always done it. The young woman then asked her grandmother, who replied, "I don't know why you and your mother do it, but I had to cut the ham because my pan was too small." A new day and a new pan size offered the young bride the opportunity to change, to transform an old way into a new way appropriate for her.

There are times when the connections with the past must be broken in order for new ways to emerge. I think of a friend who has a family history of substance abuse, primarily alcoholism and dependence on prescription drugs, stretching back several generations. She has had to change long-established patterns of how one relates in a family in order to break the cycle of substance abuse and let new and healthier patterns of relating emerge in her current family context.

It is often said that the seven last words of the church are "We have always done it that way." To avoid change leads to stagnation and death. To embrace change opens us to the present with all its possibilities and to the future with its hopes and dreams.

Continuity and change. We have here a core understanding of the purpose of educational ministry in the church. To be true to our calling to be the people of God we must educate for both continuity and change. Mary Elizabeth Moore, a noted scholar and church educator, states it this way:

> The Christian community, in all its longing for relevance and influence on the contemporary world, must recognize that its story is ancient. The same community, in its longing for the stability of long-established truths, must recognize the dynamic way in which its story is told, interpreted, and transformed.[9]

And she adds, "Both continuity and change are essential to the life of the Christian community."[10]

Those committee members who said that the purpose of Christian education is to teach the Bible and to transmit heritage were raising the issue of continuity. It is important that the Christian community pass on the Christian story. We need to know the beliefs, values, and practices that characterize that story and shaped the lives of our Christian ancestors. We need to be able to distinguish between cultural folk wisdom, such as "God helps those who help themselves," a famous quote from Benjamin Franklin, and the Christian story, which is a story of how God helps those who are least likely to be able to help themselves. We need to teach the Bible to children, youth, and adults so that we can know and claim our story and be shaped by it. We need to know who we are and whose we are.

We also need to know the unique heritage that shapes the community of faith to which we belong, whether that be Disciples of Christ, Presbyterian, Methodist, Lutheran, United Church of Christ, Baptist, and so on. There is growing concern among Protestant denominations in the United States about issues of identity. Research shows that people today seldom select a church on the basis of denominational affiliation and often have limited understandings as to the heritage that has shaped that particular community of faith.

To enter fully into the life of a community, however, we need to have some sense of the heritage that shapes and forms it. This call to continuity is not to build an exclusive church community, separated from the rest of the Christian family. Instead, it is to understand the unique identity that marks this part of the family so that we can bring that perspective to the wider Christian family and celebrate together both our uniqueness and our similarity.

But education in the church is not just for continuity. We must also educate for change. The committee member who said that the purpose of Christian education is to learn to apply the Bible to life was raising the issue of change. The gospel must be heard anew in each generation, in each setting, and in ways that speak to that day, time, and place.

Joseph Grassi talks about the need for "kingdom-centered" religious education rather than "church-centered" education.[11] Kingdom-centered education is focused on mission with and to the world, on creating *shalom*, a world of peace and justice that would truly be God's world. Such education calls for creativity and new ways of seeing and doing. Too often our purpose for educating in the church is to create good church members who will know the rules and regulations, work hard, and do things the "right" way. Instead, we need to be educating faithful disciples who live lives of Christian faith in and for the world. We are forming "Christ's ones," not "church ones." Such a formation process calls for change.

I was mindful of this need to embrace change during a visit to the Democratic Republic of the Congo (then known as Zaire) in 1991. My husband, an American Baptist minister, and I were visiting some of that denomination's mission work in that country. We were struck by the vitality of the worship services with the joyous singing and the sounds of the drums and the exuberant way the worshipers danced in the aisles to bring their offerings to the altar. We were told the story of the early missionaries who originally banned the use of drums and dancing, calling them evil. Yet these were central to the lives of the people, and slowly the realization came that drums and dancing were important to the expression of their faith. The missionary understanding of what it meant to be bearers of good news in that setting had to change in order for Christianity to take root and flourish in the lives of these people.

Daniel Aleshire, in talking about the need to learn the Christian story *both* ancient *and* present, points to the fact that the story is not held captive by ancient texts, but is alive today as God breaks forth in new ways in the world around us. As Mary Elizabeth Moore puts it,

> In the Christian community change takes place in each generation and in different parts of the globe as persons read the past from inside their own unique sociohistorical contexts and as novelty is introduced into these situations through the inbreaking of God.[12]

God is waiting to break forth in new ways into our lives. As we educate in the church, we must educate in ways that do not close us to this inbreaking of God, but rather open us and prepare us for the One who makes all things new.

Why, then, do we educate in the community of faith? We educate so that the community will be rooted in and faithful to its past (continuity) *and* open to the present and future as God calls us forth into new life (change). It is not an either/or choice, focusing on either continuity or change. It is, instead, a both/and, seeing both continuity and change as essential to the church's life and future. As Moore puts it,

> What is being said is that the more continuous we are with our past, the greater is the possibility for transformation. What is also being said is that the more we change, the more continuous we are with our past.[13]

I see this integration of continuity and change witnessed to and present in the teaching ministry of Jesus. An excellent example of this can be found in the gospel of Matthew, chapter 5. Here we find what is known as the Sermon on the Mount, one of the great collections of Jesus' teachings. It is interesting to note what he says. In verse 17 he tells the people, "Do not think that I have come to abolish the law or the prophets; I have come not to abolish but to fulfill." Jesus' claim is that he came to fulfill the law, to stand in continuity with the teachings of Judaism. Yet in verses 21 and 22, and at several other points in this section, he says, "You have heard that it was said...But I say to you..." These are words of change: You may have been taught this, but now I am teaching you this.

Continuity and change. Jesus' own ministry was marked by an ongoing call to the Jewish people to return to their roots, to the heart of their law, to the fulfillment of their teachings. Yet this ministry was clearly an invitation to change, to transformation, to living life in a new way that would bring justice and mercy to all. In our own education for discipleship we can do no less!

Summary

In her excellent book on the curriculum of the church, Maria Harris talks about the purpose of Christian education. She says that the essence of our work in education is to fashion the people of God for their pastoral vocation. In other words, as Christians we are *all* called to ministry, and the aim of our education is to equip all to respond to this call in whatever shape and form it takes. She describes it in this way:

The truth of our baptism and confirmation is confronting us regularly, and we are beginning to see that being incorporated into this people (the Christian faith community) carries responsibilities with it. No longer is it enough to be passive members, receiving a word told us by someone else, filing that word away to be taken out for a reading now and then. No longer is it enough to leave the work of the church to pastors and ordained leaders, as if the total responsibility was theirs. Instead, we are realizing that the word of God is addressing us, saying something to us, making demands on us, and asking us to live that word in our lives. We are a people called by the gospel, called to make a difference in our world.[14]

This call means that we need to be very clear about *why* we do Christian education. In this chapter we have looked at this question of purpose, and now I invite you to look at your own congregation in terms of why it educates. Even as you name your own goals and purposes, I place before you the vision proposed here, a vision that calls us to educate for continuity and change. Such a vision enables us to know who we are and whose we are, yet calls us forward into the world as ambassadors of reconciliation, able to speak a relevant word and to be bearers of hope and new life to a world so desperately in need.

Reflection and Application

The following exercises are offered to assist readers in their engagement with the ideas presented in this chapter.

1. Prepare a list of purposes that represents the aim of Christian education in your congregation. Compare your list with the purposes of the Christian education committee members, Aleshire, and Groome presented in this chapter. What is similar? What is different?

2. On a sheet of paper, newsprint, or a chalkboard, make two columns. At the head of one column, put the word *continuity.* At the head of the other column, put the word *change.* Using the list of purposes you have prepared, place each one in the appropriate column according to

whether you see that purpose concerned primarily with continuity or with change. Study the columns and discuss what they indicate about the purpose of Christian education in your church. Is it primarily focused on continuity or on change? Why do you think the emphasis is where it is? How might you want to change the emphasis?

3. Bible study:
   a. Read Matthew 5:17–20.
      (1) What do you hear Jesus saying here?
      (2) In what ways do you see Jesus in continuity with the law and the prophets?
   b. Read Matthew 5:21–43.
      (1) Note the number of times Jesus says, "You have heard that it was said...But I say to you..." What happens each time he says this? In what ways is he advocating change?
      (2) What do you think Jesus would say to your congregation about its call to continuity and to change?

4. Prepare a statement of purpose for Christian education for your congregation. Consider what you would need to do in order to implement this purpose statement in your setting. What would change in the way that you do Christian education? What would remain the same?

5. How could you share this purpose statement with the wider church? Prepare a plan of action for doing such and for receiving congregational input.

9-19-01

Chapter 3

CONTEXT:
Where Do We Educate?

"Context is everything." She spoke the words with such conviction. I pressed her further. "What do you mean?" She said again, "Context is everything. Where we do something—the physical setting, the cultural setting, the time of day—all of these influence how we educate and what people learn." The speaker was a former student who had returned to share some of her wisdom with one of my classes. Her place of ministry was a large inner-city African American congregation, and her audience in the class was primarily white suburban middle-class students. She was challenging them to be aware of the importance of context in education, to not assume that "one size fits all."

CONTEXT refers to the settings, circumstances, and situations within which a particular event or happening occurs. This third building block calls our attention to the importance of the settings and environments within which education takes place. Too often in the church we take context for granted. We presume that certain settings are "educational," mainly the church school, and seldom seem aware of the other contexts within which teaching and learning take place. The neglected physical condition of those places that we identify as educational also adds to this impression that we ignore context. I've been in too many church school classrooms that showed little evidence of any care or attention—paint was peeling; chairs and tables were broken; old papers were piled in bookcases; everything could have used a good cleaning. Nor do we seem to realize that context is more than just the physical space; it includes attitudes, emotions, relationships, cultural qualities, and many other factors that shape the environment.

We need to see the importance of context for the church's educational ministry. My own understanding of this foundational building block has been greatly helped by the work of Elliot Eisner. In his book *The Educational Imagination,* he highlights issues of context in his discussion of what schools teach.[1] He says,

> But schools teach much more—and much less—than they intend to teach. Although much of what is taught is explicit and public, a great deal is not. Indeed, it is my claim that schools provide not one curriculum to students, but three.[2]

He goes on to talk about the explicit, the implicit or hidden, and the null curriculum. The explicit curriculum refers to what is consciously and intentionally presented as the teachings of that school, the actual *content* we are teaching. The implicit curriculum is what a school "teaches because of the kind of place it is."[3] In other words, the context—the physical characteristics of the school building, the way the day is organized, the emotional environment, the way people relate to each other, and many other factors—teaches important lessons to students whether we are aware of it or not. And finally, the null curriculum refers to what schools do *not* teach. Maria Harris, in her discussion of Eisner's work, describes it this way:

> This is the curriculum that exists because it does not exist; it is what is left out. But the point of including it is that ignorance or the absence of something is not neutral. It skews the balance of options we might consider, alternatives from which we might choose, or perspectives that help us see. The null curriculum includes areas left out (content, themes, points of view) and procedures left unused (the arts, play, critical analysis).[4]

Eisner believes that the lessons the implicit and null curriculum teach, although often unintentional and unconscious, are among "the most important lessons a child learns."[5] What he challenges us to see is that the context itself teaches and therefore needs our attention.

I once heard the story of a little girl whose mother was a professional journalist and traveled a lot. The father performed most of the parenting functions for their daughter. One time the little girl was playing house. She was holding a doll, and someone asked her who she was. She replied, "I'm the father." When asked where the mother was, she said she was away writing a story. No one sat in a classroom and taught that little girl a formal lesson about how mothers work and fathers take care of children. It was her context that taught her this.

Context teaches in the church, too. Without ever saying a word, we teach what it means to be a Christian by the way we design our churches, by the way we welcome or do not welcome people into those churches, by the way we relate to each other as a church community, by who is allowed to speak and who isn't—the list could go on and on. Whether it is the appropriate lesson or not isn't the point. The point is that we are teaching something through our contexts. When only men are seen in the pulpit or in positions of leadership in the church, we are teaching something about the place of women in the Christian faith. When we remove children from the worship service on a regular basis, we are teaching them something about what it means to be a Christian. When our educational structures are designed to look like schools, we implicitly send a message about how we are supposed to learn to be a Christian.

The issue here is not that context is bad. Context is a necessary and basic part of education. The issue before us is *awareness*. Too often in the church we seem to ignore the importance of context and the key role it plays in our educating. We take certain contexts for granted (such as Sunday morning and a classroom) and assume that this is when religious education occurs. We miss all the other times and settings where education *is* occurring (such as the worship service, fellowship dinners, choir practice, a hunger walk, the home) and lose the opportunity to be more intentional about the ways in which these contexts assist us in our important task of educating disciples. It is important that we consider the building block of context, become aware of the settings we currently see as educational in the church, and give consideration to a broader understanding of context and *where* teaching and learning can and do occur in the community of faith.

Context: Sunday School

The response is almost always the same. When asked to name the first thing that comes to mind when they hear the term *Christian education,* most people say, "Sunday school." I have asked the question of students, of Christian education committees, of pastors, and of other folks, and the response is universal. The identification of Christian education with this one particular context is strong and pervasive.

Many of you reading this chapter probably responded in similar fashion. After all, some of us have been shaped and formed by the Sunday school. It is one of the primary contexts in which we have been taught about the Christian life. It has been an important setting where the Christian faith was explained and taught, shared and lived. I still name my junior high Sunday school teacher, Mrs. K., as one of the important influences in my own spiritual journey.

Originally established in the 1780s as a structure to educate working-class children in England, the Sunday school was soon exported to the United States and became a movement that played a role in the European settlement of this country. In its early years, it was an agency completely separate from the church. Only in the middle of the nineteenth century did the church adopt the Sunday school as its own agency for education.[6] Since that time it has been seen by many as the major context for Christian education.

There have been contrasting images of the Sunday school in our society. As Jack Seymour describes it,

Throughout its two-hundred-year existence, the Sunday school has meant many things to many people. For some it is the evangelistic arm of the church, for others it is the context for serious study and instruction, and for still others it is an intimate, caring fellowship. Its life has engendered deep feelings of pride and caustic criticisms. Assessments of its work have always been varied. For every positive statement made about the Sunday school, there seems to be comparable criticism...The Sunday school has inspired extremes of feeling–sarcastic criticism and inordinate praise.[7]

These contrasting images were highlighted in a 1995 edition of *Church Educator* magazine when two articles about Sunday school appeared in the same issue. One was titled "Sunday School is *Not* the Answer," and the other dealt with "Growth Dynamics for Growing Church Schools."[8] Clearly there are mixed feelings about Sunday school as a context for Christian education.

Whatever we feel about Sunday school, it *is* a part of the church's educational environment and, in many churches, provides a needed setting for introducing the Christian faith to the largest possible number of children, youth, and adults. It can also be a setting that provides important nurturing for people. There are Sunday school classes that become a "church within the church." I have witnessed this particularly in the lives of aging members of a congregation whose Sunday school class provides much of the needed pastoral care as they face the reality of loss of spouses and of the limitations that aging brings to physical capacities. My own family experienced this reality as we watched my mother's Sunday school class minister to her in deeply caring ways when my father died.

I believe we need to value this context for what it does and what it provides. It has been, and continues to be, a place of nurture for many people. It continues to provide an introduction to the faith for many. It is an accepted part of the educational ministry of many congregations. As D. Campbell Wyckoff says, we need to "respect the Sunday school for what it has been, what it is and does and for its potential future contribution; provide it with appropriate backing and fitting resources; and promote it realistically, claim for it neither more nor less than it can produce."[9]

Rather than continue to debate the merits of Sunday school, I invite us to accept it as a given. It is an established context that provides us with a time and place in the church for education. As Wyckoff suggests, we need to be realistic about what it can and cannot do as a context for religious education. We can't teach everything a person needs to know to be a faithful disciple in fifty minutes on Sunday morning. But we can provide some basic content. We also need to commit some resources to its work. Too often I hear of churches trying to solve a budget crisis by eliminating money for education, specifically Sunday school. If this context is to be effective, we need to provide resources for it, including both money and people.

In working with this context for Christian education, however, we must also remember that "the Sunday school was never called to do the whole task of Christian religious education."[10] The early leaders of Sunday school saw this context as only one of several within the church where people were shaped and formed in their faith journeys. Worship, preaching, Wednesday night Bible study, women's society, and fellowship times were all seen as important parts of the whole. There was even an understanding that the contexts that worked together to help educate people in the Christian faith went beyond the church walls. Referred to by Robert Lynn as an "ecology" of religious education contexts, this wider collection included revivals, church publications, the public school, church agencies and societies, denominational colleges and seminaries, and the family.[11]

There are signs that this broader ecology has broken down and no longer provides the same widespread environment within which people are formed in the faith. Even within the church walls, we seem to have turned primarily to Sunday school as the chief context for educating Christians. Regular and ongoing Bible study, apart from the brief time available during the Sunday school hour, is disappearing from many church calendars. Women's groups committed to study and service no longer hold the place of prominence they once did in church life. Even fellowship times seem fewer and farther between as churches compete with the busy lifestyles of many of their members.

Although this old ecology has broken down, it is still important that we recognize the need for a variety of contexts, a broader base of environments and settings within which the educational ministry of the church takes place. The pervasive identification of Sunday school as synonymous with Christian education becomes a barrier to a broader vision. When "we equate Christian education with something that happens in a 'Christian education wing' of the church building, at a certain time on Sunday morning,"[12] we have greatly limited our ability to recognize and use the wide variety of contexts available for the education of Christians. I believe that our call to educate and prepare Christians for living and serving in the world today challenges us to broaden our understanding of context and become aware of the multiple settings within which we teach and learn the faith. We need to create the best Sunday schools that we can. But we need to do more.

Context: A Wider Perspective

Hear, O Israel: The LORD our God is one LORD; and you shall love the LORD your God with all your heart, and with all your soul, and with all your might. And these words which I command you this day shall be upon your heart; and you shall teach them diligently to your children, and shall talk of them when you sit in your house, and when you walk by the way, and when you lie down, and when you rise. And you shall bind them as a sign upon your hand, and they shall be as frontlets between your eyes. And you shall write them on the doorposts of your house and on your gates. (Deut. 6:4–9 RSV)

As I mentioned in chapter 1, I find many insights about education in this passage, one of my favorites in the Bible. In these words from Deuteronomy we hear not only *why* we are teaching–to help people learn to love God with their whole selves–but we also see some clues as to *where* we are to teach, which is just about everywhere. The writer challenged our ancestors in the faith to teach diligently and to do this by talking about this commandment in their homes and when they were engaged in the wider world (walking "by the way"). They were to keep these words before them in everything that they did, which meant that they were constantly engaging with this commandment, learning what it meant for their lives, and living accordingly. I call that education!

The whole of the biblical story suggests a broader understanding of context than that which seems to be operative in the church today. Schools are not mentioned in the Bible, nor would schools as we know them have existed at that time. What our ancestors in the faith seemed to understand was that the whole of life provided a context for educating. This is particularly evident when we look at the New Testament and make note of the places where education, or leading people forth into the Christian life, took place. Jesus was especially creative when it came to context. Although we see him teaching in a synagogue (Lk. 4:31–37), we also find him teaching by a well (Jn. 4:1–42); on a mountain (Mt. 5:1–11); in a home (Lk. 10:38–42); during a banquet (Lk. 5:29–39); on a boat (Mk. 4:35-41); in the fields (Lk. 6:1-5); and on a walk (Lk. 24:13-35). It appears that our Christian story invites us to broaden our perspective when it comes to the settings and environments in which we educate.

What are some basic insights about context that can help us to broaden our perspective regarding this foundational building block of educational ministry? Though the following is certainly not an exhaustive list, let me name three such insights:

1. It is the whole life of the congregation that teaches.

This first insight calls us to see that it is the *congregation*, the whole church, that educates. It is not just those people called "teachers" working in places called "classrooms" who are educating. It is the total life of the community of faith, life that is lived both inside and outside the walls of the church building. Everything we do as a congregation teaches what it means to be a disciple of the Christ.

Maria Harris, a noted religious educator, provides us with some important perspective in this discussion about the congregation as a context for education. In her book *Fashion Me a People*, she talks about five basic ways, or "forms" as she calls them, through which the community of faith shares in life together. These forms include *koinonia* or fellowship, *leiturgia* or worship, *didache* or formal instruction and teaching, *kergyma* or proclamation, and *diakonia* or service and mission.[13] Harris sees each of these as contexts in which we are "fashioning," or educating the people of God.

In other words, education in discipleship occurs not only in the context of formal instruction in a church school classroom, but also in the midst of fellowship, whether we are gathered for a potluck supper or participating in a family camp. It occurs in the context of worship, whether it is a Sunday morning service or a devotion time during a committee meeting. Education takes place when we are proclaiming the gospel, whether it is giving testimony during a service or voting as a church to take a stand for justice on a particular issue. And we learn about being Christian through the context of service, whether we are building a house for Habitat for Humanity or sponsoring a walk for hunger. In each of these contexts, education is taking place, and people are being formed in their faith.

The challenge for the church is to pay attention to each of these contexts. Remember our discussion earlier in this chapter about the implicit curriculum? Everything we do as a congregation and every place we do it *is* educating, whether we are aware of it or not. It seems to me that if we are going to take seriously the context building block of educational ministry, we will start with an awareness of all the places and settings within which we interact as a community of faith. We will look at our worship services, our fellowship times, the mission and service projects in which we engage, the committee work we do. We will become aware of what is already being learned through all these settings and how these learnings do or do not help people grow in their discipleship. We will become more intentional about what happens and how it happens in each of the contexts of congregational life, knowing that in all places and in all ways we are forming the people of God.

2. There is more than meets the eye in a given context.

Certainly what we see when we walk into a particular context (be it a church school classroom, a sanctuary, a church camp fellowship hall, or wherever) immediately tells us something about the identity and values of that community of people. Broken furniture, crumbling plaster, musty smells, and dirty floors send a message about what being a Christian means in this place. The presence or absence of symbols (e.g., a cross, banners, candles, pictures) and even the arrangement of chairs or pews communicate a vision of the Christian life in implicit ways. We certainly need to attend to these important physical characteristics of a context, but, as the old saying goes, there is more here than meets the eye. Other characteristics of context beyond the physical need our attention.

A. EMOTIONAL AND ATTITUDINAL NATURE OF CONTEXTS

The first of these is the emotional and attitudinal nature of the contexts within which we educate. I often hear people talk about how they "feel at home" in a particular place, or don't "feel safe" in a certain setting even when there is no clear evidence of physical threat. I think at these moments people are talking about the emotional and attitudinal qualities of a context. Paying attention to these qualities is as important as attending to the physical condition of a particular space.

Space where we feel unwelcome, feel afraid to express who we are and what we believe, or feel threatened by those who seem to hold power is not space where much learning can take place. In such an emotional environment we are too busy trying to protect ourselves to really be open to learning and growing. The sad thing is that such space is not unknown in the church. I have been in congregations where I have not felt welcomed, not because people said I wasn't wanted, but because they did nothing to include me. I have sat in church school classes afraid to speak my beliefs for fear of being ridiculed or put down by both teacher and students. And the ridicule does not have to be obvious. It can be as subtle as the teacher rolling his or her eyes when someone begins to speak, as though to say, "There he goes again." These are not moments or places where much helpful learning takes place!

What helps to shape good emotional and attitudinal space, space where learning is enhanced? I believe there are at least three key qualities of such a space. These are hospitality, openness, and a sense of safety.[14] Hospitality refers to the act of receiving others with an attitude of warmth and care; it means to make people feel welcome. In educational contexts, it also means to welcome new thoughts and ideas. We encourage people to share different perspectives and views and to receive these, not as threats, but as opportunities to learn and grow. The biblical tradition is rich with images of hospitality, of welcoming the stranger. As the author of Hebrews says, "Do not neglect to show hospitality to strangers, for by doing that some have entertained angels without knowing it" (Heb. 13:2). As we seek to learn and grow in our Christian faith, an attitude of hospitality opens us to the new work God may be wanting to do in our own lives, both personally and as the church.

The quality of openness calls our attention to the need for a context marked by an attitude of freedom and mutuality. People feel free to share what they are thinking and feeling, to ask questions, to wrestle with hard issues without fear of attack or ridicule. Open space calls us "to remove the impediments to learning that we find around and within us."[15] One of the impediments often at work in educational settings is the fear of appearing ignorant. It makes it difficult to say, "I don't know," or "I don't understand." Yet learning begins with the ability to say, "I don't know, but I would like to find out." Another impediment I see at work in the church is what I call "authoritarianism," the need on the part of some clergy, educators, teachers, and parents to be the authority and have all the right answers. They create contexts where there is little freedom to explore, to differ, or to try out new ideas. In such a context, learning is certainly limited, if not blocked altogether.

A sense of safety is the final quality I want to mention. We hear a lot about "safe space" in our world today. As a society we struggle daily with the violence that has moved within the very walls of our schools and public places, onto our highways, and within our homes. I believe that it goes without saying that physical violence simply has no place in the community of faith, as it should have no place in the wider society. But there are other ways we do violence besides the physical, and these need our attention too. When we belittle a person, make fun of him or her, or respond with sarcasm and ridicule, we are perpetuating violence, and there should be no place for this in the educational contexts of the church. Contexts where we seek to nurture disciples must be considered safe spaces, free from violence of any kind, shaped instead by grace and loving care.

B. The Cultural Nature of Contexts

"Learning is always done in a cultural context."[16] With these words, Ella Mitchell reminds us of the importance of culture in our educational efforts. The contexts within which we educate are always shaped by the culture within which they are rooted. A congregation located in a small, midwestern farming community settled by German immigrants does not share the same cultural context as a large, urban Chinese American congregation located in a major West Coast city. There are present within each of these settings certain perspectives on the world, certain understandings of who people are, and certain patterns of teaching and learning that seem natural and appropriate. What "works" educationally in one setting will not necessarily be useful in the other. Again, we have to set aside our one-size-fits-all perspective in order to educate in ways that will engage people and help them grow.

Mitchell suggests that different communities have always used "cultural vehicles"[17] to assist them in their teaching tasks. It is when we overlook these culturally sensitive approaches that we can find ourselves struggling in the educational task. In an example from her own cultural context, Mitchell suggests that the African American church loses some of its educational vitality when it relies too much on printed material and forgets one of its central cultural vehicles, that of storytelling, a teaching tool rooted in the rich oral tradition of the African community.

To use stories and illustrations primarily from city life when working with children in a farming community is to ignore the significance of cultural vehicles. To have only pictures of European Americans on the walls of a Sunday school classroom in a Chinese American congregation is to ignore the significance of cultural vehicles. When we are sensitive to the cultural nature of our contexts, we will look for those cultural vehicles that can engage people where they are and enable them to hear the gospel and its meaning for their lives and to grow in faith.

3. Context stretches beyond the doors of the church building.

As was noted earlier, it is the whole life of the congregation that teaches. We now expand on this truth to note also that a congregation not only shares life within the walls of a given church building, but also experiences life as a scattered people beyond the doors of the church building. Sometimes it is easy to overlook the life beyond the church and forget that this life also provides us with contexts for educating in faith. In fact, I propose that two of the most important, yet often overlooked, contexts for Christian education are located outside the church walls. These are (1) the home and family and (2) mission and service.

"For better or worse, our families have more influence on our character, values, motivations, and beliefs than any other institution in society, including churches and schools."[18] For all our efforts in the church, family religious experiences are key to our children's faith development, and research indicates that family religious activity within the home seems to be declining from one generation to the next.[19]

We hear lots of reasons for the family's neglect of religious education within the home. With busy schedules, both parents working, and so many activities for both adults and children, there simply doesn't seem to be enough time in the day. It seems that the days when families shared most of their meals together, with time for grace before and conversation about all kinds of topics during, are gone. The important religious holidays like Christmas and Easter are lost in a sea of commercialism that few families seem able to overcome.

However, I don't want to make this a "blame the parents" issue. I think that the church has played a role in this decline of religious activity within the home by ignoring the importance of the home and family as a context in our religious development. A friend of mine is a minister to families and children in a local church. One of the constant concerns parents bring to her is their struggle with talking about faith issues with their children. They don't know what to do or how to do it, and more often than not, the church has not helped them in their task. The most popular events she holds are those workshops where she works with parents on such topics as how to pray with children, how to answer those difficult questions only children can ask (like, did their pet cat go to heaven when it died?), or how to explain, in a way a child can understand, the meaning of important theological concepts like baptism, communion, resurrection, and so on. She also finds parents wanting help on how to make Christmas and Easter meaningful religious holidays rather than the commercial icons they have become.

When we expand our vision to those contexts outside the walls of the church building, we see the home and family as a vital setting for Christian education and know that we need to work at engaging this context in creative and meaningful ways. It begins with the acknowledgment that when a baby is born, the parents do not receive a manual that tells them how to go about the religious education of this child, even though they will be their child's primary religious teachers. They need help and assistance from the very beginning, and the wider church can be there, providing guidance and helping parents create a setting in their home for the religious nurture of their child.

An example of how we might approach this in the Christian community can be seen when we look at what those in another religious body are doing. The Central Agency for Jewish Education in the St. Louis area has developed a program called "Our Jewish Home," which seeks to address the issue of parents as religious educators.[20] Based on the Missouri Parents as Teachers program, this effort at claiming the home as a primary context for religious education uses trained lay teachers who work with parents of preschool children, going into the home to help parents learn prayers, special rituals, songs, and other activities that they can use in the home to help teach and preserve their Jewish heritage. The families also take part in group educational activities with others in the program. I believe that, with a little thought and effort, local churches, perhaps joining with others, could draw on this idea. They could develop programs appropriate for their settings that would take seriously the home as a context for Christian education and provide the resources to help parents and extended families in their efforts.

The other context that moves us beyond the church walls in our educational efforts is the context of mission and service. I think we would all agree that the church is called to be in mission and service in the world. But I'm not sure that we often realize that the mission and service in which we engage are also important contexts for teaching and learning.

I believe there is little argument that experiential education is a vital educational model. It is one thing to be told about something, to be given facts and information. It is quite another to actually engage these facts and information and learn how to use them. For example, we can talk all we want in a church school classroom about feeding the hungry; but we move to another level of learning by actually being involved in a feeding ministry and encountering the poor and hungry in our own neighborhoods. In the church we need to move beyond seeing our mission and service as simply ways to "do good" and also claim these contexts as important settings for learning about what it means to be a disciple of Christ.

A new model of teaching and learning that has recently found its way into both the public and religious education arenas is a model called "service-learning."[21] It is an approach to education that seeks to understand and use service as an important context for learning. Rather than understanding service as just things that we do to help others, this educational process also sees service as a way of learning and an avenue for growth and development. Because research supports the claim that service that is undertaken not only for the purpose of doing good but also as a means of learning *does* help persons grow and mature in their faith,[22] it seems vitally important that the church see beyond its walls and acknowledge mission and service as a context for Christian education. It needs to involve its people in such contexts and seek not only to serve, but to be intentional about the learning that can occur.

Summary

In many ways, I feel that I have been stating the obvious in this chapter, but often it is the obvious that we have ceased to see. Like driving a familiar route to home or work, we stop "seeing" the scenery. The same thing happens with context. Because we take it so for granted, we stop seeing this important aspect of educational ministry and reflecting on it. When we fall victim to the "tyranny of the obvious," we lose the ability to select and shape the contexts of education in ways that truly assist the teaching and learning we want to happen.

While context may not be everything, as my former student claimed, it *is* a vital factor in our educational efforts and a building block to which we must attend. Contexts *do* teach, and the condition and quality of our educational contexts *do* matter. In the church, we need to think about the contexts we use, beginning with the church school but moving beyond to see the breadth and depth of contexts available to us for nurturing people in the growth of their Christian identity. As we expand our vision of *where* educational ministry occurs, we expand the opportunities we have to teach and learn, to grow in wisdom, and to become the disciples we are called to be.

Reflection and Application

The following exercises are offered to assist readers in their engagement with the ideas presented in this chapter.

1. Drawing on examples from the chapter and adding others that you think of, make a list of all the contexts for Christian education that you see your congregation using. With this list, do the following:
   a. Put a check mark by each of the contexts that you believe the majority of the congregation would clearly identify as a context for Christian education.
   b. Put a minus sign (-) beside each of the contexts that you believe the majority of the congregation would not clearly identify as a context for Christian education.
   Study the list. What does it tell you? What might be done in your congregation to increase awareness of the importance of context and of the variety of contexts available?

2. Make a list of those contexts for religious education that you believe your congregation is not employing or using in any intentional way. What would it take to begin engaging those contexts? What could you, as an individual or a committee, do? What would be a first step? What would need to follow that first step? Outline a brief strategy for engaging new contexts in your particular congregation.

3. Take a walking tour of your church facility, doing this as a group if at all possible. Before starting the

tour, imagine that you are a first-time visitor and know nothing about this congregation, perhaps even know little about Christianity. Enter this experience with all your senses open, being as aware as you can of what is around you. The following suggestions are offered to guide your exploration:

a. Begin at the point where a person would first come in contact with your facility, maybe a sign down the street or the entrance to the church parking lot. Take note of your surroundings. What do you see and hear? What do the surroundings suggest to you about this congregation, its identity, and its understanding of itself?

b. Enter the building by whatever door is convenient. Again, pause and take note of this spot. What do you see? How does it seem to welcome you? What and how do you feel as you approach it? What does it seem to say about the congregation's understanding of itself and the people who come here?

c. Move slowly through the building, making note of signs and symbols and ways in which you are directed through the space. Pause regularly to note what you are seeing, hearing, feeling. Limit talking among the group as much as possible so that you can focus on the impressions. Feel free to enter rooms, to sit in chairs or pews, and to experience the environment as fully as you can.

d. As you move through the building, keep asking the following questions:

(1) What does being a Christian seem to mean in this place?

(2) What does context seem to tell you about these people? What seems to matter to them? What seems to be overlooked?

When the tour is complete, gather as a group and discuss the following:

i. What was this experience like? What did you notice? What did you learn about context?

ii. Think about the qualities of hospitality, openness, and safety. How would you rank the space you just toured in terms of these qualities?

iii. Think about the cultural nature of space. What "cultural vehicles" for teaching and learning about Christianity did you see present in the space?

iv. What have you learned about context, and how would you go about sharing these learnings with the rest of the congregation?

Chapter 4

CONTENT:
What Do We Need to Know?

I hear two questions repeated with great regularity in the church, especially in the late spring or summer when churches are planning for the new church school year to begin in the fall. They are: "What topics are we going to study?" and "What curriculum are we going to use?" These are questions of content, of what we will teach, study, and learn in the community of faith. CONTENT is a crucial aspect of the educational ministry of the church, certainly a key foundational building block that needs our attention and consideration.

Although we deal with content on a regular basis in Christian education in the church, generally using the language of "curriculum" in our discussions, I am concerned about how much careful thought is given in a local congregation to this important building block. As with the other building blocks we have discussed, we often assume that there is a common understanding of content and that we all agree on what it is and what we need to be studying and learning. Yet I believe there are some myths about content at work in the church, myths that confuse and cloud our understanding. Let me name four such myths.

1. *Content has to do with facts and information.* One of the myths I see operative in the church is that content is only about facts and information. I notice this myth at work when I hear members of a congregation talk about the need for the children and youth to "know the Bible." If pressed, I discover that they are talking about the need for these young people to know the "information" that the Bible contains. The emphasis is on

the words on the pages, on memorizing verses, on being able to recite the Ten Commandments, the Lord's Prayer, the names of the books of the Bible, and so on.

This definition of content emphasizes the cognitive, the importance of *knowing about* something. As with many myths, there are seeds of truth here. It is important to know about the Bible; but if we limit our understanding of content to just the cognitive, to acquiring only facts and information, we miss the importance of feelings and attitudes, what we call "affective" knowledge. We also miss a vital part of content for the Christian community, the behavioral dimension of our knowing. We not only need to know about the Bible, but also how to embody its truths and insights in our own lives, in other words, how to live as Christians in the world today. For example, it is one thing to know *about* Jesus' admonitions in Matthew 25:31–46 to give food to the hungry, drink to the thirsty, clothing to the naked, and so on. It is quite another to know *how* to do it in our own communities. Limiting our vision of content to just facts and information limits our opportunities to learn and grow as disciples of the Christ.

2. *Content is a set of curriculum resources.* Mention the word *content*, or use the more familiar term *curriculum*, in the church and chances are you will conjure up "images of boxes piled on top of each other in out-of-the-way places, packed with dull workbooks for children to fill out endlessly in Sunday school."[1] When I raise questions of content with seminary students or with local churches, more often than not the conversation begins with a discussion of what printed, published resources they are using. When asked what they are studying in their church, people generally reply, "Oh, we are studying *The Inviting Word*," or "We use *Bible Discovery*." In other words, they name the curriculum resources they use. I seldom hear the following: "We are studying what it means to be disciples of the Christ in the world today, and some of the resources we are using are…" I think the reader can hear the difference.

The presence of this myth can limit our ability to see what it is we need to study, or, as the title of this chapter reminds us, what it is that we need to know. In our discussion about context in chapter 3, we talked about the challenge Maria Harris offers the church to broaden its understanding of the contexts in which we educate. I think she also challenges us to broaden our understandings of what content is and to see beyond the limits of printed resources. As she says, "It is *the entire course of the church's life*"[2] that educates, and we find content–things we need to know–throughout the life of the church. We need to know what worship is and how to do it, what proclamation is and how to do it, what it means to serve, and how to be in community together. All of this is the content of educational ministry.

As with our first myth, there are seeds of truth in this myth, too. The resources we use are a part of the content we study, and we need to select these through careful thought and effort. We will look at this in greater detail later. What we need to realize, as all good teachers know, is that it is not the curriculum material that teaches, and it is not the resources that determine content. Resources are simply a tool to help us study and learn what we need to know.

3. *The Bible is the content that really matters.* "We've got to teach the Bible." I hear this statement over and over again in the church. I heard it when I interviewed church school teachers as a part of my doctoral research. Telling Bible stories and teaching about the Bible were the central concern of these teachers. As one teacher said, "I think probably the most important thing is to make sure...these children...are knowledgeable about the Bible."[3] This suggests an implicit belief that the Bible is the subject matter that really matters, and that if we are teaching *about* the Bible, we are doing our job.

Please don't get me wrong. I believe that the Bible is very important subject matter in the local church. We need to know the story that shapes our core identity as Christians. It is content that calls for our faithful and full attention. To ignore the Bible as a central part of the content we need to teach is to put the future of the Christian community in jeopardy. But to limit our content to only the Bible prevents us from helping people come to the fullness of knowledge needed to be committed and faithful disciples in the world today.

Anne Wimberly reminds us of some of the other important "subjects" we must study in the church in her discussion about "story-linking," a model of Christian education growing out of her African American church context.[4] She talks about three kinds of stories that need to be brought into dialogue, linked together, in the educational ministry of the church. People need to study their own life stories, to know what has helped to shape and form them. They need to study their heritage stories, to know how their particular racial and ethnic context and their particular denomination's perspective shapes and forms them. And finally, they need to study the Christian story in scripture to know the vision of who we are called to be as disciples of the Christ.

What Wimberly helps us to see is that *people* are important subjects in the educational ministry of the church. It is the *people* of God we are helping to fashion and form. Their everyday experiences and stories, their cultural heritage and its stories, are all a part of the "many layers"[5] of subject matter and should be seen as important aspects of the content of Christian education. Whether they study the Bible with the care we would like, the children in our churches do study the lives of the people around them, and they learn from those lives what it *really* means to be a Christian in that community of faith.

4. *Content is the concern of Christian education committees and church school teachers.* This myth shares much in common with another myth related to Christian education in general: "Christian education is separate from the rest of congregational life."[6] The Search Institute study, discussed in the Introduction, discovered evidence that many congregations see Christian education as unrelated to the other aspects of congregational life such as worship, committee meetings, coffee hours, potluck dinners, service projects, and so on. I believe a similar perspective is at work with regard to content, and on the whole we relegate questions and issues of content to Christian education committees and church school teachers. It is not that these committees and teachers are not concerned with content; but to limit our discussion of this significant building block in this way does not serve the church well.

I recall my service on a worship committee of a local congregation some years back. During the year I was on this committee, we certainly dealt with what I consider to be important content questions, like what hymns to sing, what litanies to use, how we would include children in worship, and so on. But we did not talk about what we were doing in terms of the broader issue of content, of what it is that we need to know as Christians. When we selected a hymn, it was generally evaluated as to whether it fit the theme for that Sunday or not. We did not ask about the content of the hymn in terms of what it "taught" us about our Christian walk. We seemed to miss the point that, whether we were intentional or not, people would gain knowledge and insight about what it means to be a Christian from the words of those hymns, from the language of the litanies, from their participation in the worship experience. My hunch is that most of the members of that committee, if asked to think about content, would reply that it was the board of Christian education's responsibility to make content, or curriculum, decisions. The worship committee planned worship.

If Maria Harris is right, and I believe she is, that the whole life of the church is educating people in their faith, we must see that decisions about content and what is to be studied, taught, and learned are not just decisions for Christian education committees and church school teachers. We are educating in worship, service, fellowship time, committee meetings, and all the other myriad forms of congregational life. That means issues of content should be raised in all these contexts, too. What are we learning through our committee work about what it means to be Christian? What are we learning as we fellowship together? Content, what we need to know as Christians, is the concern of the whole community of faith.

The list of myths I have just named is not meant to be exhaustive of the false perceptions regarding content that are present in the church today. I encourage you to think about your own setting and the myths that you see operative there. What is important is the naming of these myths in order to help us see them at work in our own congregations. Once we recognize them, we then have the opportunity to move beyond them and look at this building block of content to consider the issues it raises for our work in education in the church.

Issues of Content

As I look at issues of content, two significant questions come to mind that should be explored as we consider what to teach and study in the church. These questions are: (1) What do we need to know? and (2) How do we need to know it? Both of these questions are at the heart of the educational task of the church.

1. What do we need to know?

I see them used with some frequency in the church. They are surveys designed to discover what the current issues in people's lives are and, therefore, what they want to study in the coming year. This kind of "issues-based" approach determines the content of Christian education by taking a poll and then studying whatever it is that people say are their current issues and interests. Another approach I've seen used is what I call the "theological disciplines" approach. This strategy for determining content turns to the classical disciplines of theological education and says that subjects such as church history, theology, Bible, and ethics are to be studied. A third approach is one I call "the Bible" approach. I see this in churches who claim the Bible as the only content. In this approach, scripture, and scripture alone, is the one thing worthy of study.

As these approaches suggest, there are a variety of ways in which we can decide the content of our Christian education. It seems to me, however, that the starting point for determining content needs to be the question, What do we need to know? In order to claim the identity of a Christian and live as Christians in the world, what is it that we need to know?

I believe that each of the approaches mentioned tries, in its own way, to answer this question. The issues-based approach says that to be a Christian you need to know about life issues and how to relate your faith to them. Therefore, we begin with the people we are educating and seek some understanding of their issues and concerns. These become important entry points into opportunities for learning. The theological disciplines approach says that we need to know information about history, tradition, and the theological debates in the church. Such an approach does remind us that education in the church is a serious matter and that laypeople need to be challenged intellectually and invited into conversation with the major thinkers and scholars and with core theological concepts that have shaped and formed their tradition. The Bible approach says that we need to know the Bible. It reminds us that scripture is a key part of the content of Christian education and that we neglect it at our peril.

All these are certainly appropriate areas of knowledge for a Christian to explore. If we look at the definitions of Christian education that we discussed in the first chapter, we can see some other ways in which this question about what we need to know is addressed. Remember Thomas Groome's definition:

> Christian religious education is a political activity with pilgrims in time that deliberately and intentionally attends with them to the activity of God in our present, to the Story of the Christian faith community, and to the Vision of God's Kingdom, the seeds of which are already among us.[7]

Clearly, Groome is naming some categories of content, what it is that we need to know, when he calls for education in the church to attend to (1) "the activity of God in our present," (2) "the Story of the Christian faith community," and (3) "the Vision of God's Kingdom." In other words, we need to know about God's activity in our present, what it is, how to recognize it, what it means, and so on; we need to know the Christian story, both in scripture and tradition; and we need to know what God's vision for the world and humanity is and how to embody that in our lives.

Daniel Aleshire's definition also offers a perspective on what it is that we need to know:

> Christian education involves those tasks and expressions of ministry that enable people (1) to learn the Christian story, both ancient and present; (2) to develop the skills they need to act out their faith; (3) to reflect on that story in order to live self-aware to its truth; and (4) to nurture the sensitivities they need to live together as a covenant community.[8]

The Christian story, skills to act out our faith, awareness of the relationship between the story and our lives, and sensitivities for living together as a covenant community are all areas of knowledge, things we need to know about and/or how to do in order to live as Christians.

Although these approaches and definitions are certainly not exhaustive of the possibilities, each provides a perspective on ways in which we can name the content of our educational ministries. I offer them not to advocate for one over the others but to provide you, the reader, with some awareness of the ways in which we can think about the content that we will teach and study in the church. As Eugene Roehlkepartain suggests, perhaps our goal should not be to name one of these as more important than the others but to look for a "helpful balance,"[9] one that sees effective content as incorporating a variety of information and facts, interests and life issues, core theological concepts, and scripture.

My goal in this discussion about different ways of naming content is not to push for the development of a "normative" curriculum for the church, for determining the "right" things we need to know. I believe that many of us would agree on the general areas of knowledge and understanding that should be explored in the church. Included would be areas such as God and God's activity in our lives, Jesus and his ministry, the Bible and the Christian story, the church and its mission, our own cultural and religious heritage stories, an awareness of other cultures and religions, what it means to live as a Christian today, the disciplines of the Christian life, and so on.

My purpose here is to challenge us to *think* about this question of what we need to know. We need to be encouraged in the church to broaden our approach to selecting content, to move away from looking only at the issues of the people or to the classical fields of theological study or to the Bible alone or to any single criteria as a way of determining what will be studied. The knowledge needed to live faithfully as a Christian in today's world is multifaceted and multilayered. It calls for a broad and inclusive approach when selecting content. My purpose is to invite you and your congregation to *talk about* what it is a Christian needs to know and to examine your own educational ministry to see the scope of what is being taught and studied, and what is being ignored.

2. How do we need to know it?

What it is that we need to know is certainly a central factor in selecting the content of our educational endeavors. However, equally important to the question of *what* is the question of *how*. How do we need to know it?

Too often in the church we work out of a limited understanding of what knowledge is. We see knowledge as "propositional,"[10] in other words, as knowing *about* something, or knowing *that* something is thus and so. Much of our work with the Bible in the church is propositional knowing. We emphasize the knowing *about* and the knowing *that*. When we push children to memorize Bible verses, we are often engaged in propositional knowing. Our goal is that they know that John 3:16 is this particular set of words and that they are able to recite those words.

Nothing is wrong with propositional knowing. We do need to know about things. It is important that we know what the Bible says. It is important that we know about God and Jesus and the church. We need to provide people with information about their faith. But there is more to knowing than knowing about. A philosopher of education, Jane Roland Martin, states the issue this way:

> Education is not and ought not to be limited to learning *about*: there are skills to be acquired, techniques to be mastered, activities to be learned, works of art to be appreciated; there are emotions to be fostered, attitudes to be developed, convictions to be encouraged, ways of acting to be promoted.[11]

Her words remind us that just knowing *about* something is not enough. Knowing about Jesus and his life and ministry is certainly important, but we have not fulfilled our educational obligations in the church until people know *how* to witness to that life and ministry in the world today.

This question of how we need to know invites us to examine the content that we choose and to realize that this content cannot be limited to just knowledge about something, to just knowledge found in study guides and books. We also need content that explores knowing *how*, knowledge that comes from lived experience and the opportunities to engage in new behaviors, practice new attitudes, and feel different emotions. The service-learning approach to education, mentioned in the previous chapter, takes seriously this need to know how and involves people in the kind of hands-on experience that leads to a fullness of knowing that is vital to the community of faith. Engagement in lived experience, with its opportunity to learn how as well as about, is a foundational aspect of content for the educational ministry of the church.

Even though I did not realize it at the time, my seventh-grade church school teacher, Mrs. K., taught me the importance of emphasizing knowing how as a part of the Christian education experience. We were a group of girls, most of us raised in the church. We knew our Bible verses from all those summers spent in vacation Bible school. We had learned our lessons about how Christians were supposed to serve others. We had a lot of propositional knowledge, knowledge about, but Mrs. K. taught us something about knowing how. Rather than talk about what it meant to serve others, she introduced us to Grandma P., an elderly woman confined to her home. She was blind, hard of hearing, and showing signs of diminished mental capacity. We "adopted" Grandma P. as our class grandmother. As a group we went to see her on several occasions, made and sent her small gifts, and prayed for her regularly. Suddenly, service took on a new dimension and meaning in our lives. Service wasn't some abstract idea that we learned about in church school. It was the hard work of finding things to say to Grandma P., of confronting our own discomfort in being with someone who did not respond in the way we imagined she would. The content of our religious education became a knowing how as well as a knowing about.

Thomas Groome says it well: "The fool or ignorant one in the Bible is not the person who does not 'know about' intellectually, but rather the one who fails to do God's will."[12] As we consider the content that we will teach and study in the church, we need to ask ourselves, How do we need to know it? We need to know it with our whole beings, know it in ways that we can respond in faithfulness to the will of God in our lives.

Selecting Resources

Althoug it is vital that the church move beyond the myth that sees content simply as the curriculum resources we use, the resources we select are important tools for helping people learn the content that we believe is important. Even though we know that resources don't teach and that the selection of curriculum materials does not complete our responsibility with regard to the content of Christian education, to quote a proverbial wisdom, we don't want to "throw the baby out with the bathwater." Curriculum materials are important, as a part of the content we study, and we need to select them with careful thought and effort. Therefore, a brief discussion about how we go about selecting these resources seems in order.

This is also a stewardship issue for me. Over the years, I have seen denominations spend millions of dollars on the development of new curriculum materials and their promotion in the church. The newest materials become the focus of the moment, and churches spend money in acquiring these new materials, believing that these resources will be just what they need. Pretty soon, teachers begin to grumble, students don't seem to be interested, and we begin the cycle all over again. Old curriculum materials pile up in church supply closets, and we wonder if it will ever end.

I do not want to criticize denominations and their efforts in developing useful curriculum materials. We need good resources, and I am grateful to those who give time and energy to their design. But we do need to pause and recognize the amount of money that has been spent over the years on the repetition of this cycle and to ask ourselves if this is the best use of our financial resources. Are we being good stewards of that which we have been given? Is developing new curriculum materials always the answer? Is there something we might do to keep from repeating this cycle so often?

There is something we can do. We can engage in a deliberate and intentional curriculum resource selection process that will help us become better stewards in providing the resources needed to assist people in learning what they need to know. While I do not believe that this is a totally new suggestion to many of you, it bears repeating again and again in order to encourage the church to engage in serious efforts with regard to this important issue of selecting materials. Let's take a closer look at one way we might shape such a process.

Curriculum Resource Selection Process

Like Iris Cully, I do not believe that there is "one easy way"[13] to go about selecting curriculum resources. However, I do believe we can take some steps that will help us engage in this important work with some intentionality, giving it the kind of thought and effort it deserves. As I have worked with seminary students and churches, a set of five important steps has emerged as basic to the selection process. I name them as follows:

- Prepare the ground
- Describe the particular situation
- Select the resources
- Use the resources
- Evaluate the resources

1. *Prepare the ground.* When I talk about the process beginning with a "preparing of the ground," I am drawing on the image of gardening. My husband is a dedicated gardener, and one of the important things I have learned from him is the necessity of preparing the ground, adding nutrients and working the soil so it is ready to receive and grow the plants. The result of such preparation is a beautiful flower garden in bloom throughout the season.

When selecting curriculum resources in the church, we also need to prepare the ground, to help the church get ready to select the kinds of materials it will use. The discussion about content that we have been engaging in throughout this chapter is a preparing of the ground. It is helping people remove some of the myths and false perceptions (like removing rocks and weeds from the soil) that can inhibit a broader understanding of content. It is helping them gain a new vision, looking at what it is that we need to know as Christians and how we need to know it. It is helping to prepare the way for the selection of resources appropriate to the task.

This working of the ground is an ongoing task. Like the good gardener whose efforts in preparing the soil are never complete, we need to regularly discuss issues of content and look at who we are as Christians and what it is that we need to know. We need to keep new myths and false perceptions from sprouting or the old ones from returning. We need to return again and again to prepare the ground.

2. *Describe the particular situation.* Before looking at specific resources, we need to describe the current situation. Again, it is like a physician making a diagnosis. She would not write out a prescription before taking the time to know who we are and to listen to us describe our symptoms. I believe that the same is true when selecting curriculum resources for use in the church. We risk making the wrong selection when we have not taken the time to describe the setting, the church, the people involved, what we need and want to learn and how, and so on.

We need to do two kinds of description in this phase of the selection process. The first is a description of the congregation and context in general. This includes describing who the people are, their needs and interests, where they are in their Christian journeys, what kinds of Christian education experiences they have had, how they seem to learn best, and so on. This also includes a description of the ways in which the congregation responds to the questions raised earlier in this chapter about what Christians need to know and how.

The second kind of description is a more focused one related to the curriculum resources themselves. In this descriptive task, we need to name the qualities that we look for in a resource, qualities that would help it be a fit for our particular congregation and its educational work. For example, there are churches that demonstrate a strong preference for a particular Bible translation. To use a Bible study resource that did not use that translation at all would probably not be a good fit and could quickly lead to dissatisfaction with that resource.

Besides the choice of Bible translation, other factors important to consider are ways in which your church likes to study the Bible (topical, lectionary, verse-by-verse, etc.), the educational approaches your teachers seem to prefer (lecture, discussion, projects, lots of hands-on crafts, etc.), the actual conditions under which the resources will be used (length of time for the study sessions or classes, number and age range of students in a given group, etc.), the role that denominational heritage, mission, and values should play in the resources, and the kinds of aids for teaching that your teachers and students expect (teacher's book, student book, craft materials, take-home papers, etc.). Although certainly not exhaustive of the factors that we need to explore, this list gives an idea of what we need to consider and describe as we prepare to select the resources we will use.

3. *Select the resources.* Obviously, the steps already mentioned are a part of the selection process, but there comes a point when we have to choose, to actually decide on particular resources. This process begins with the gathering of a variety of possible resources. There are several sources for discovering what is available: church resource centers, denominational publishing houses, religious bookstores, other churches, and so on. My recommendation is that a church have more than one set of resources for review. This provides the opportunity to examine different approaches and offers some comparison for evaluation purposes.

After the materials are assembled, those responsible for the decision need to evaluate them. I encourage people to use the descriptions developed above as they do an initial screening of the materials. How well do the descriptions and the materials seem to match up? Following this overview, I suggest a checklist, like the following that I have developed for use with seminary students and congregations, for a more detailed analysis of the materials.

An Evaluation Checklist for Selecting Curriculum Materials[14]

OVERALL DESIGN OF MATERIALS:

1. What are the stated goals of this curriculum material? How appropriate are these goals for your church's approach to Christian education? Are they similar to the goals that you have set for teaching/learning?

2. Content:
   a. Is the material what you want to study?
   b. Does the biblical material reflect an acceptable approach to biblical interpretation?
   c. How appropriate is the material in terms of its interpretation of the meaning of the Christian life?
   d. Is the content appropriate for the students in terms of age level, developmental issues, learning abilities, and life experiences?

3. Arrangement of the material:
   a. How is the biblical material used? What are the advantages and disadvantages of this approach to the scriptures?
   b. What is the structure of each session? How are the sessions related to each other? Is this an appropriate structure for your setting?
   c. Is there space for additions and substitutions where appropriate? Are there suggestions for such additions and substitutions?

4. How would you rate the material in terms of its physical appearance? Its usefulness in terms of the skills and preferences of your teachers? Its overall appropriateness for your particular students?

5. Can your congregation afford this material? Can it be used again?

TEACHER MATERIALS:

1. Is the format of the material attractive?

2. Are the sessions clearly outlined so that a teacher can easily understand the movements of teaching? Are there particular features that help the teacher understand the outline and its progress?

3. What kinds of teacher helps are provided? Are these appropriate and useful?

4. How well does this material match your teachers' skills?

5. What approaches to teaching are used? Are these appropriate? Are instructions for activities clear and easy to follow?

6. What resources are suggested for use beyond those provided? Which of these are essential? Which ones could be easily obtained?

7. Is helpful material about the ages, learning levels, needs, and interests of the students provided? Is there background material about the content so that the teacher's knowledge and understanding will be enriched?

STUDENT MATERIALS:

1. From the student's perspective, is the material attractive? Is the printed material easy to read? Does the style and language attract the student's interest? Is the material within the student's understanding?

2. How are the students engaged in the learning process? Are they engaged in ways appropriate to their ages, learning abilities, needs, and interests?

3. What kinds of activities are used? Will the activities attract their interest? Will the students find these activities useful? Are these activities appropriate to the content?

CONCLUDING QUESTION:

Weighing the advantages and disadvantages, would this be the most appropriate and useful curriculum material for your church? State your reasons.

After having used a checklist such as this, the decision is finally made about the actual resources that are to be used in teaching the content we have determined is foundational to the Christian faith.

4. *Use the resources.* Too often in the church we think that our task of selecting resources is completed when we have made the decision about what materials we will use. Because of this,

churches end up repeating the step of actual selection over and over again because it is not understood that this is only part of the process. After materials are selected, we need to see that they are used and to provide the appropriate support and assistance for this to occur.

But this does not always happen in the church. I recall a comment made by a teacher I interviewed in my doctoral research. She said, "They just hand you a book and say 'Here's your material. Go teach.'"[15] She was voicing the concern of many of her colleagues in teaching that little help was given in using the resources. As was said before, it is not the resources that teach; it is teachers who teach. And we need to give them assistance in using the tools we provide.

Helping teachers to use the materials can be addressed in a variety of ways. A novice can be paired with an experienced teacher who is able to offer insight and provide some mentoring in the use of the curriculum materials. Churches can conduct a workshop that focuses on helping teachers become familiar with, and learn to use, the resources selected. I know we hear all the time that teachers don't have extra time to give, but my own experience says that teachers will come to a one-time, focused event when they see that it will benefit the actual work they are called to do.

At issue here is not the way in which we provide help in using the materials. At issue here is the realization that we have not successfully selected curriculum resources until those resources are being used. I believe that careful and deliberate attention to this step will go a long way toward eliminating those piles of unused curriculum materials found in many church supply closets.

5. *Evaluate the resources*. The curriculum resource selection process is brought to conclusion with an evaluation of the resources as they are being used. Evaluation occurs any time we ask the question, How are things working? We may do this through informal conversations with teachers, students, parents, and anyone involved in the educational endeavor. We may do this through the use of surveys to see how people are responding to materials, what they like and don't like. We may do this by asking students questions to see what they are

learning. The point is not the method used but the need to engage in some type of evaluation of the resources and their usefulness.

I believe that the selection process is not complete until we do this evaluation. Yet it is a step that can be overlooked. My observation is that evaluation often happens at a point when problems have already developed, and it is then more difficult to make wise choices about what to do. If we wait until a teacher complains or students stop coming, we may have waited too long to address the question, How is it working? By that time the answer can quickly become that it isn't working, and pressure develops to cast these materials aside and find others. Checking at an earlier point and on a regular basis offers greater flexibility in making whatever adjustments may need to be made to help a resource be useful. It can help to prevent the costly replacement of resources.

This cycle—preparing the ground, describing the particular setting, selecting the resources, using the resources, and evaluating the resources—is not a process we do once and for all in the church. It is one that we need to visit again and again. It may not always result in choosing new resources; in fact, I would hope that it would not. However, it will result in the presence and use of appropriate resources that assist the congregation in teaching the content to which it is committed.

Summary

If the reader approached this chapter looking for a discussion of *the* particular content that needs to be taught in the church, I am sure he or she is disappointed. As I have already said, the purpose of this discussion about the foundational building block of content is not to name a normative curriculum for the church or to dictate the specific things that people need to know. I believe that this falls into the trap of the one-size-fits-all mentality. I have not tried to outline a general, all-purpose curriculum for the church.

Instead, my purpose here, as it has been throughout this book, is to raise an _awareness_ about the issues a church needs to address when it is making decisions regarding what it will teach.

We need to consider the core questions, What do we need to know? and How do we need to know it? and we need to answer these in the context of our own particular congregational and cultural settings. Although resources should not be equated with content, we also need to give some careful and considered attention to the selection of appropriate materials for use in our educating.

My hope now is that this discussion becomes a springboard for your church to consider how it will name what it believes is important for Christians to know and then to shape the content of its educational ministry accordingly. I invite and encourage you to deliberately and intentionally pay attention to this basic building block and to seek to make decisions regarding it that are appropriate for your particular community of faith. May your knowledge increase!

Reflection and Application

The following exercises are offered to assist readers in their engagement with the ideas presented in this chapter.

1. List the four myths about content on a sheet of paper or newsprint. Rank these myths from 1 to 4, number 1 being the myth that you most often see at work in the church and number 4 being the one least evident. Add to the list other myths that you have seen at work. Name some ways in which you could begin to dispel these myths.

2. Imagine you were designing a "school for Christians."
   a. Make a list of what you think people would need to learn in this "school." What do Christians need to know? Indicate which of the items on your list could be categorized as a knowing *about* and which ones as a knowing *how.*
   b. Make a list of what is currently being taught and studied in your own congregation. (Remember to think broadly and not limit your thinking to the formal classroom setting.) Indicate which items on the list are a knowing about and which ones are a knowing how.

c. Compare the two lists. What is the same, and what is different? What do you learn about your own church's approach to content as you look at these lists?

3. Select some curriculum materials already being used by your congregation. Using the Evaluation Checklist for Selecting Curriculum Materials, evaluate these materials.

   a. What do you see about the materials that you did not notice before?

   b. How would you rank the materials? Are they useful for your congregation or not?

4. After having used the checklist, look at it again.

   a. Which of the criteria do you think are most important?

   b. Which criteria were most helpful in evaluating the materials?

   c. What criteria would you add to the list? What criteria would you delete?

Chapter 5

PARTICIPANTS:
Whom Do We Educate?

The faces always draw their attention. Spread out on the tables in front of them are pictures of people, people of all ages, races, sizes, and shapes. Even before class begins, they pick up the pictures and study them intently. Who are these people? What's this all about? You can see the questions forming in their minds. The students in my introductory course in Christian education are about to begin a discussion of the "who" in this important ministry, and spread before them is a collage of those whom we are called to educate.

As we think about that collage of pictures and the question of this chapter, Whom do we educate? the first and most obvious response we can give is, Everyone. We educate old and young, male and female, rich and poor, black and white, professionals and blue collar workers—the list could go on and on. Christian education is a lifelong process involving people across the life span. In spite of that all-too-prevalent myth in the church that education is only for the young, the participants in educational ministry range from the cradle to the grave.

Yet there is so much more to this question than the obvious response of "Everyone." Who are these "everyones"? PARTICIPANTS, the fifth of our foundational building blocks for Christian education, invites us to take note of the people we educate and to ask what it is that we need to know, what it is that we need to pay attention to with regard to them. This building block calls us to remember that people are at the heart of this important ministry, people created in the image of God and called to be disciples, called to care for and serve each other and this world in which we live. Our task is indeed a holy one and challenges us to become aware of who these people are and to discover what we need to know in order to faithfully educate them. As Craig Dykstra says in his foreword to Daniel Aleshire's book *Faithcare*, "Many factors are included in good teaching and pastoring, but at their heart lies the ability to be receptive to others, to understand, pay attention to, and discern with some clarity how life is experienced by those in one's educational and pastoral care."[1]

Paying attention to the people we educate is basic to our educational task. Yet it is too easy to pay attention to certain aspects of people and therefore think that we know and understand them. Think about the conversation that you have when you meet a person for the first time. More often than not, these conversations begin with the sharing of names. Then they move to the question, Where are you from? followed closely by, What do you do? Name, geographical location, and job are the aspects of a person to which we seem to give our initial attention. In addition, we are taking note of their gender and physical characteristics. Unconsciously, we begin to categorize them—male or female, tall or short, blond or brunette, child or adult, Southerner or Northerner, teacher or engineer, and the list goes on. We then begin to make judgments about them based on these categories and the assumptions we make.

My concern is that we often limit our understanding of people to these judgments and to the preconceived notions we tend to hold about certain groups—"Oh, those are just those junior highs! They are always rowdy." We miss the rich complexity and unlimited variations that human beings really are. My purpose in raising the question of this chapter is to invite us to move beyond this kind of surface attention to people and to think carefully about what it is we need to know in order to educate with care and faithfulness in the church.

So what do we need to know about these participants? What kind of information and understanding will be especially useful to us? Although the following are certainly not exhaustive of all that we might find helpful, let me focus our attention on three areas of understanding that I believe can be of great benefit to us as we seek to faithfully educate the people of God. These are (1) an understanding of the complex and multidimensional nature of being human, (2) an understanding of human development, and (3) an understanding of how people learn.

The Complex Nature of Being Human

There is a funny story told about two neighbors. Let's call them Pete and Sam. Both Pete and Sam were retired and spent a lot of time in their yards and often fell into conversation with each other. One day Sam was complaining about something one of the children in the neighborhood did. Pete immediately chastised him for being so critical. After all, kids will be kids. Pete went on to talk about how much he loved children and about how they were our future. A couple of days later, Sam was in his backyard when he heard loud voices coming from the front. Going around to see what was happening, he saw Pete standing at the end of his driveway, yelling in an angry voice at a group of children who were obviously running to get away. Sam said, "Pete, what's going on? I could hear you clear in the back. Calm down and tell me what happened." Pete, pointing to some newly laid concrete at the end of his drive, said, "Those kids were playing ball and look, one of them hit it right into my new concrete and left a big hole. Kids today are so careless. They run wild. They don't care about other people's property." The tirade went on and on. Finally, Pete paused for a breath and Sam spoke up. "But Pete, you were just telling me the other day about how much you loved kids." Pete sputtered in an angry voice, "Well, yes, I love kids—but in the abstract, not in the concrete!"

We chuckle at such an obvious play on words. Yet Pete has spoken some words of truth. From my observation, it is much easier for us to think of people in the "abstract," in the kind of generalities that give us a false sense that we understand them. We do it all the time in the church. We talk about the sixth-grade boys, the toddlers, the senior adults, those junior highs mentioned earlier. We behave as though that label tells us something about the people in that category. And the truth is, it does. It just doesn't tell us all that we need to know.

When thinking about human beings and seeking to understand who they are, we need to remember that there are at least three kinds of characteristics that identify any one person. There are those universal human qualities in which we are just like every other human being. We all breathe air, need water, feel sad, need love, and so on. Then there are those group-specific qualities in which we are like some other persons and not like others. The categories mentioned above—sixth-grade boys, toddlers, senior adults, and so on—are an example of this kind of grouping. Finally, there are those unique individual qualities that make each of us not like anyone else. For example, though we all need food to live, we each have our individual preferences with regard to the food we eat.

The universal and group-specific categories can be helpful to us in trying to understand people, who they are and what they need. It is important to know that everyone needs love and that toddlers share certain characteristics. But we need to remember the truth that our friend Pete was struggling with. People come in the "concrete." Each human being is particular and unique. Each human being is complex and multidimensional, and we are called to pay attention to this if we hope to educate in meaningful ways.

Keeping in mind that each person is particular and unique, we need to pay attention to some aspects of being human as we work at our educational task. There are some things we need to make note of as we contemplate these "whos" that we educate. I call these "perspectives on human beings." I like to use the image of a lens when I talk about these various perspectives. I believe that they provide us with a lens through which we can view a person and come to some insight about who they are, what their life issues might be, and how they grow, learn, and change. I see four such perspectives as useful for our discussion here. They include the biological, psychological, cultural, and theological natures of humans.

Biological

The first perspective from which to view human beings is that they are biological creatures. This means that each of us is a living organism shaped and formed in certain ways. We come in a particular sex (and there *are* differences between males and females); we have certain physical abilities and limits; we have lived a certain number of years; and we are maturing physically in certain ways. Because of our biological development, we are able to do different tasks at different times in our lives. A child of one is not yet able to tie her shoes, but that same child at four is often delighting in that ability. Although I do not believe that biology is destiny, it is certainly something that we need to remember as we seek to educate.

I became aware of the importance biological factors play in teaching and learning when I recently taught a class of older adults at a local church. During the course of our weeks together, I became mindful of the need to regularly check to see if they could hear me and whether they could see the chalkboard on which I was writing. Because of the size of the room, some of them had to sit at enough distance from the chalkboard that it was difficult for them to see. I found making copies of some of my notes and enlarging the print in the copies, too, was helpful for their learning process. Research shows that both sight and hearing decline with age, and to ignore this in our educational experiences with older adults prevents them from enjoying the fullness of learning. Although the capacity to learn does not decline with age, the natural losses in hearing and seeing can affect the learning process.[2]

Biological factors affect the learning process no matter what the age. We know that sleep deprivation can influence a teenager's ability to pay attention. We know that lack of adequate nutrition can affect a child's ability to engage fully in a learning experience. Paying attention to the biology of those we teach and to what is happening to them of a physical nature is important for our work of education in the church.

Psychological

The second perspective from which to view human beings is the psychological one. Psychology looks at the emotional and behavioral characteristics of a person. Using the psychological lens, we are encouraged to be attentive to the personalities of the people we educate. We take note of the different ways in which people relate to the world and to each other. We become aware of the different ways in which people respond to the situations in their lives. Although we all have access to a variety of responses and behaviors in our "psychological toolbox, each of us is more comfortable with, and thus prefers, a particular tool (or set of tools) for a particular task."[3]

This need to attend to the different personalities among my students has been a helpful insight in my own teaching. To illustrate, through the years I have observed that some of my students are more quiet, tend to not speak a lot in class, and like to sit back and reflect on issues for a while. Others are quite talkative, have their hands up almost before the question is out of my mouth, and tend to dominate the class discussions. There is nothing wrong with any of these students; they just have different ways in which they engage the world. As an educator, I need to attend to each of these. I need to allow the quiet students time for reflection and make room for them when they want to enter the dialogue. I need to allow time for discussion for the more outgoing ones and help them focus their thoughts. I need to help each of them learn to appreciate the other and what each brings to the conversation. Attending to the psychological nature of human beings is also important as we go about our educational task.

Cultural

The cultural perspective is the third lens that provides us insight about the people with whom we work. Who we are as persons is influenced and shaped by our culture. Our families and communities, the environments within which we grow and develop, help to form in us a particular identity. We acquire certain manners and traditions, certain values that tell us how to live and relate in the world. We learn particular ways of behaving, of interacting, even of seeing the world. And we come with our particular cultural perspectives to the learning moment.

One of the ways that we acquire our cultural identity is through the constant repetition of folk wisdom that we hear over and over again. As a child, I can remember hearing with some regularity the statements "Children should be seen and not heard" and "Children should speak only when spoken to." It wasn't very difficult to translate these cultural "wisdoms" into my early educational experiences and to feel that I should be quiet in class and speak up only when I was called on. Learning to voice my opinion and become more vocal in class took some effort, and I was helped by teachers who were sensitive to the cultural values I held and hindered by those who were not.

Ella Mitchell, in her work on the cultural nature of education,[4] talks about the importance of cultural sensitivity when working with people. She points to some of the problems she sees in educational ministry in many African American churches and attributes some of this to a lack of attention to the cultural qualities of that community. She believes that the black church was too quick to adopt the style of the white Sunday school and forgot some of the key cultural values of its own community, most importantly its powerful oral tradition. What she calls an "exaggerated fascination with print"[5] that marks the larger culture has become a barrier to engaging African Americans in the significant art of storytelling that is deeply embedded in that culture's traditions. We must attend to the cultural nature of those we educate if we are to be faithful in our work.

Theological

People are not just their biology, their psychology, and their culture. As Christian educators we claim that there is another perspective that is vital to our human identity, a theological perspective. This final perspective on human beings that I want to highlight calls us to give thought to the biblical and theological understandings of what it means to be human and how these understandings shape our educational work.

As Christians we believe that we are created in the image of God, made to be "a little lower than God" (Ps. 8:5). But we are also told in scripture that we are finite, limited creatures, sinners, little more than dust (Gen. 3:19). The apostle Paul claims that we have gifts (1 Cor. 12) and are called to develop these and exercise them on behalf of the church and the world. Yet he also acknowledges that we are only "clay jars," susceptible to cracking and being broken (2 Cor. 4:7). The biblical image of what it means to be human is certainly complex and richly layered.

The importance of naming this perspective grows out of my belief that the way we see ourselves from a theological and biblical point of view influences our educational work whether we are aware of it or not. If we see humans as only sinful and depraved in nature, it becomes easier to turn our educational efforts into indoctrination. We *have to* put the right thoughts into these students; we *have to* make sure that they behave properly; we *have to* instill the "fear of the Lord" in them. We must stay in control at all times, and rules and regulations become very important in our educational settings. However, if we are able to see that humans, while limited, fallible, and sinful, are also created in the image of God and are full of potential and possibility, we are free to explore, question, try new things, and be open to the Spirit's movement in our midst. It is important that we give careful thought to the theological and biblical perspectives that we hold with regard to the people we educate. Such perspectives will shape how we do our educational work.

Being aware of the complex nature of the "whos" we educate is vital to our ministry. We need to attend with care to the particular, unique nature of each person in our community of faith. We need to note the various factors, like biology, psychology, culture, and theology, that shape and influence each person in his or her growth and learning. In so doing we are able to make a place for all persons as we teach and learn in the church.

Understanding Human Development

Human beings develop. They do not come into this world "fully growed," as my grandmother used to say. They change and grow across a lifetime. In order to effectively educate the participants in our educational ministry, we need to have some understanding of human development. Although it is too complex a subject to deal with in depth in this overview of Christian education, there are some important issues regarding human development and our approach to it that I want to raise for your awareness and thought.

We certainly have available to us a variety of theories of development that provide insight into how people grow and change. Particularly, Jean Piaget's theory of cognitive develop-ment, Erik Erikson's theory of psychosocial development, and James Fowler's work in faith development are all helpful to those working in educational ministry in the church.[6] I encourage readers to explore these various theoretical approaches. However, my purpose here is not to focus on a particular theory, but to look at the developmental perspective in general and to consider what we need to keep in mind about this perspective when working with the people we educate.

It is important to remember that development of any kind should not be seen as an unchanging pattern, a particular set of stages that are followed in invariant order, a kind of one-size-fits-all process. While many theories, called "stage" theories, describe the different steps or stages that people tend to follow in a particular developmental process, we need to remember that people don't always grow in such a linear, logical, step-by-step manner. There are twists and turns on our journeys that don't always fit the theory categories.

Because of this, I believe it is important to see develop-mental theories as *descriptive*, as tools that help us to describe what might be happening in a particular person's life at a par-ticular moment. We are using such theories descriptively when we *begin with the person* and observe particular behavior and responses. For example, we may note that a child is starting to think logically and deal with abstractions, and we can then turn to Piaget's theory of cognitive development to gain some insight into the child's developmental progress and how we might assist in that.

The problem comes when we try to use these theories in a *prescriptive* manner. We do this when we *begin with the theory* and its categories and try to fit people into them. We use a theory prescriptively when we say that such and such a theory says this about two-year-olds; Johnny is two; and therefore, this is what Johnny is like. And if he isn't, something must be wrong.

When we use developmental theories *prescriptively*, we tend to become judgmental with them, to use them as a way to see whether someone is "measuring up" to a certain standard, or fits a certain mold. If the person doesn't, then we begin to think that there is something wrong with that person, and we place labels that can be very damaging to the individual. We label children as "slow," or "underdeveloped," and they become marginalized by such labels.

However, when we use developmental theories *descriptively*, they become a tool that can help us to understand what may or may not be happening on a person's developmental journey. But the theory does not dictate who the person is. Instead, we start with the person and who he is. We don't try to fit him into a particular box. This gives us greater freedom and flexibility to actually assist people in their own unique development and to provide the help and resources that they might need.

I trust that the reader can see that whatever theoretical approach we take, *how* we use the theory is critical. In addition to how we use the theories, other important understandings about the developmental process are significant for our work with the participants in educational ministry. I like to think of these as *principles* of development that provide us with a perspective on the whole developmental approach. Let me name four such principles.

1. *Development is a **multifaceted** process.* This principle should be obvious, but it bears highlighting here. Simply put, this principle of development reminds us that development has many facets or "faces." We don't develop in just one aspect of our lives. We are growing and changing in the whole of our being. As humans, we develop biologically, psychologically, socially, cognitively, in our faith journey, and so on. It is important in the educational ministry of the church that we see and understand these many facets of development and attend to them in our work. We cannot focus just on faith development and forget that the other facets are present and influencing our efforts. This leads logically to the next principle.

2. *Development is a **connected, interrelated** process.* The various ways in which the human person develops—biologically, cognitively, psychologically, socially, and so on—are connected and related to each other. None of these aspects of development occur in isolation from the others. I'm sure that

many of you have heard of studies done regarding infants who, for various reasons, are left in isolation, not held or touched or talked to. Even though they receive adequate nourishment and physical care, they still fail to thrive, and many die early deaths. It seems clear that their biological development is related to their psychological and social well-being.

It is important that we realize that humans are whole, integrated beings. In our educational work it is vital that we not isolate one aspect of a person's development and ignore what is happening in the whole of her life. While we want the children, youth, and adults in our church to be able to think carefully about their faith (cognitive development) and grow in it (faith development), we also need to pay attention to what is happening in their homes and families, whether they feel safe and affirmed as persons (psychological and social development), and whether they are adequately fed and their physical needs are being met (biological development). All these are working together to help sustain and nurture an individual's growth in faith.

3. *Development is **multi-influenced**.* There are many things that shape and influence our development in all its many facets. Both our biology and culture play a role in how we develop. This means that our growth is shaped by those genetic givens with which we are born *and* by the environments within which we live. While this nature/nurture question has been debated hotly through the centuries, the evidence seems to be clear that it is not an either/or, but a both/and. The world around us, the situation facing us at any given moment, and our internal biology all play roles in how we develop.

What is essential is that we remember that there are many influences at work in the lives of those we educate, and it is important that we pay attention to these various influences. When a person's development seems to be hindered, we may discover a factor, like a violent home environment that works to prevent a child from being able to trust others, that we can play a role in changing. At other times we may need to help a person accept a given about who they are, like a child from a family of musicians who shows absolutely no musical ability, and help him come to value and appreciate himself as a unique child of God with his own gifts to share with the world.

4. *Development is* **modifiable**. This final principle brings a great deal of hope and possibility into our work in education. What it says is that everything is not predetermined and pre-set from birth. What it says is that development is not a rigid, inflexible process that we have to watch run its course as we simply stand on the sidelines. What this principle calls us to remember is that God is at work in the world, seeking to bring about transformation and new life, and we can rejoice in that. We can also claim our call to play a role in this transforming work of God and make a difference in the lives of those we teach.

This principle calls us to take a second look at the teenager who we think is impossible and will never change. It challenges us to explore ways we might reach that adolescent or find some-one who can. It asks us to be like Jesus: to look beyond the surface, to believe that people can change, to see the possibil-ity that someone like that rough and gruff fisherman Peter could actually become a leader of people. Human development is a dynamic and changing process, one that brings hope and sur-prise to our educational work.

How People Learn

I have a friend who has his own business building comput-ers. One time he related the story of a client, an older man whose children had finally convinced him to enter the com-puter world. This man asked my friend to build him a com-puter. The friend did so and took it to the gentleman's home to set it up. They had been working for a while, helping the man become familiar with how the computer worked, when the gentleman paused and stared at the screen with a look of awe on his face. He finally turned to my friend and, with a tone of hushed reverence in his voice, said, "How do it know?"

How do it know? How do *we* as humans know? Science tells us that our brains are more complex than the most com-plicated and highly developed computer. So how can we even begin to comprehend how people learn? The longer I explore the subject of how people learn, the more I, too, stand in awe of the rich complexity of the human learning process and won-der, *How do it know?*

But learning is at the core of education, and, therefore, it is important that we have some understanding about how people learn. Again, this is a topic too complex to cover in depth in this overview and introduction to Christian education. My purpose here is to raise awareness about the learning process, to offer some insight into how learning occurs, and, hopefully, to encourage the reader to explore further this important topic for education in the church.[7] Our discussion begins with a quick look at the human brain and some of the implications for education that come from our understanding how the brain works. We then move to a brief consideration of the learning process itself and the insight this holds for our work with the "whos" of educational ministry.

The Human Brain

"The human brain is the best organized, most functional three pounds of matter in the known universe."[8] Science is making rapid strides in helping us understand how the brain works and is adding daily to our knowledge about learning. Consider the following information about the brain and the resulting implications for how we teach and learn:

- Our brain has 100 billion neurons (nerve cells) plus ten times as many glial cells (support cells). How many is 100 billion? There are about 100,000 hairs on the average head, so the number of neurons in your brain would be equal to all the hairs on the heads of a million people. All these brain cells are very small and highly interconnected. This one fact alone points to the reality that the brain is a very complex organ designed to process all kinds of data and make connections among the variety of information it perceives. In essence, what science is discovering is that our brains are naturally designed to learn. Learning is going on all the time in those we seek to educate. Our task as educators is to shape the learning, but it is not up to us to make it happen.

- The brain is very "plastic," meaning that it is adaptable and changeable. We are discovering that the physical structure of the brain changes as a result of our experiences. What this means is that we can change the way the brain learns through the experiences we use in education. This helps to explain why some teachers are beginning to say that children today learn differently than they used to. The use of computers and the growing exposure to multimedia experiences is actually reshaping the brain's structure. Renate and Geoffrey Caine, in their excellent book on teaching and the human brain, quote a Hebrew proverb: "Do not confine your children to your own learning for they were born in another time."[9] The implication is clear: We must be open to new ways of teaching and presenting information in our churches' educational programs.

- Although there are significant differences between the left and right hemispheres of the brain, as early research discovered, the growing evidence is that these two hemispheres are "inextricably interactive"[10] and that the brain needs to be understood as a *whole* organ capable of simultaneous processing in multiple ways. What this means for education is that we need to teach in ways that engage the whole brain. When working with a Bible story with children, we not only need to help them learn the basic information about the story (what we might call the parts of the story), but we also need to help them enter the story and experience it as a whole. Activities like drama and role play are ways to immerse them in the story and help the brain engage in whole-brain learning.

- The brain engages in a process called "downshifting"[11] when we feel threatened or are under stress. In essence, we downshift into the reptilian brain, that part of the brain designed to help us maintain our bodies and physically survive. When this happens, the brain's capacity to learn is reduced, and our ability to engage in creative work is limited. Educationally, this suggests the importance of relaxed and safe environments where people will feel challenged to think and grow, but not threatened to do so.

This is but a taste of what is being discovered about the brain and how it learns. My hope in sharing these brief pieces of information is that you will see the significance of understanding how the brain learns for our educational work in the church. My challenge is that you discover ways to teach that work with the brain and enhance learning.

How We Learn

In the novel *A Woman's Place,* Marita Golden tells the story of three black women, Crystal, Serena, and Faith, and their efforts to claim their own identities. There is a point in the story where Faith is talking about her struggles in college. She voices the following complaint: "I just wish there was more than one way to learn what it is they want us to know. But it's all got to come out of a book and it's all got to be given back on a piece of paper."[12] The problem Faith confronted was the misconception that we all learn the same way. The truth is that there is more than one way to learn, and to educate faithfully in the church we need to be sensitive to this truth.

Each of us approaches learning with our own unique learning style, that consistent pattern of behaviors by which we perceive and process data and experience from the world around us and then make meaning of it. Our learning styles are shaped by a myriad of factors, among them our particular hereditary makeup, our personality, our particular life experiences, and the demands of the learning situation within which we find ourselves. However they are formed, we each tend to have our preferred approaches to learning.

While we have our own preferred style, the learning process itself is formed by two basic elements: (1) how we *perceive,* become aware of, and receive data, information, and experience from the world around us, and (2) how we *process* that data and information, work with and integrate it into meaningful knowledge. The differences come because we prefer different ways of perceiving and processing.

A discussion of how we perceive data immediately takes us to our five senses. Our senses are a primary channel through which we take in data and experience the world around us. One of the ways we can understand some of the differences in learning styles is to note how we engage these senses.

Waynne James and Michael Galbraith studied groups of students to see how they approached learning and discovered that they tended to group themselves into certain categories related to the sensory channels they preferred to use when learning.[13] They name seven such categories of learners in their research:

1. VISUAL: Persons who prefer their visual sense tend to learn through observation. They need visual stimuli such as pictures, charts, graphs, tables, and demonstrations they can watch. These are people who need a map rather than written directions when they are trying to locate a place.

2. PRINT: James and Galbraith discovered a distinction in those who preferred their visual channel. Some people seem to learn best through seeing the visual symbols we call words printed on a page. These folks are very word oriented and learn best through reading and writing, working with printed words. They easily retain information that they read. These are people who find written directions more helpful than a map.

3. AURAL: A person who has a preference for his or her aural channel learns best through listening. They easily retain that which is presented verbally. These are people who actually like listening to lectures, and it is easier for them to remember something they hear than something they read.

4. INTERACTIVE: Similar to the visual and print distinction in the first two categories, James and Galbraith's research discovered learners who need to verbalize out loud and to do it in the company of others. These people need to talk things out and discuss them. More than just a listening experience, something in the interaction helps them to learn.

5. HAPTIC: These are those individuals who perceive their world best through their sense of touch. A haptic learner is someone who has to feel, touch, and handle objects. They can't just listen and watch; they have to touch. Often these people need to reach out and touch

others as they are talking with them. Their educational experiences need to be as "hands on" as possible.

6. OLFACTORY: One of the interesting channels for learning that James and Galbraith name is the olfactory channel. These are people who seem to learn best through their senses of smell and taste. They can often vividly associate data and information with particular smells and tastes. This leads me to imagine what it would be like for these learners if they could smell the baking bread when learning about communion and participating in it.

7. KINESTHETIC: There are those in our midst who approach learning best through movement, with their whole body engaged in the experience. Even when having to sit and listen, a kinesthetic learner will often have some part of the body moving, whether it is a swinging foot or a hand doodling on paper. I wonder sometimes if many children who are labeled as hyperactive are simply kinesthetic learners caught in a school system that limits their use of this channel in learning.

We need to remember that people generally are not limited to just one of these as their preferred learning style, but integrate two or more into their particular approach. Our styles may also vary according to what it is we need to learn. What is important to note here is the variety of ways in which people perceive or take in the data and information from the world around them. It is vital in the church's educational ministry that we be sensitive to this and find ways in which we can help people learn in the ways that are engaging and helpful for them.

Just as there are different ways people go about perceiving the world around them, there are also different ways in which people will process the information and experiences they have. To return briefly to our discussion about the human brain, research has discovered that there are at least two different and complementary ways in which the brain processes information. One way is logical, linear, step-by-step, and analytical. This way of processing tends to focus on the parts of something rather than the whole. It notices the trees rather than the forest. This way of processing works at learning sequentially, moving from one point to the next in a linear fashion. The other way is more intuitive and processes information simultaneously, almost at the snap of a finger. This way of processing looks at the whole rather than the parts. It notices the forest rather than the trees. It works at synthesizing rather than separating and is good with visual images.

Each of us tends to prefer one of these ways of processing over the other. Some of us work better when things are presented in a logical, sequential manner. Others can absorb simultaneous images and make sense out of them quickly. What is important to remember here is that the brain engages both forms of processing, and we risk inhibiting learning when we overlook either process in our educational endeavors.

In addition to these approaches to processing, there are also different behaviors we engage in when we are working to make sense and meaning of our life experiences. David Kolb, in his research on learning styles,[14] identifies two primary behaviors. The first of these is *reflection.* Kolb discovered in his research that some people processed the data they received through reflection and observation. These are people who tend to sit back and observe, reflect, think about it. They are often initially quiet in discussions and can appear to be unengaged. But their inner dialogue is usually quite active. Their processing is going on through inner reflection and observation.

There are others, however, who immediately engage in action with regard to the data they perceive. Kolb calls this behavior *active experimentation.* These are the people who very quickly begin talking in a discussion, who will be the first out of their chairs to engage in an exercise, who will begin taking a test before reading all the directions or instructions. They process through *action* and doing.

When we think about how people learn, we need to pay attention to these different ways in which people process the data and information they receive. Some people will be more logical and linear in their approach. Some will be more intuitive and spontaneous. We will see both reflection and action used as behaviors for processing experiences. Our challenge as educators is to teach in ways that engage the whole person, that draw on all these approaches to processing. We will then be helping people to learn in ways that are appropriate and useful to them.

The "catch-22" in all this is the tendency of those who teach and educate to do so in ways that are compatible with their particular learning style. In other words, we teach to our own learning styles. After all, this is the way we learn, and we just assume that others learn the same way. The invitation to those of us who teach is to expand our own approaches to learning, to explore other ways of perceiving and processing, and thereby open up possibilities for learning on behalf of those whom we educate. Even with this very brief and limited look at how we learn, it is my hope that the reader will see the need to honor the different ways in which people learn, to be sensitive and open to this in their educational work, and to make sure that there is a place at the educational table for everyone in the church.

Summary

People are at the heart of our educational ministry. Old people and young people, men and women, people with disabilities, people of many cultures and backgrounds, people with many interests and needs, hopes and dreams. I was thinking about this chapter on participants recently as I sat during worship in a congregation with which I had become familiar across time as I provided some leadership in their Christian education program. I looked at the people around me and thought about some of the stories I knew. There was Edith, a woman in her eighties who was heroically fighting the cancer that threatened her life. There were Paul and Terry, a couple who recently adopted their second child from eastern Europe and face many challenges in nurturing that new life. There was Bill, a high school junior struggling with the recent suicide of a friend. There was little Emily, full of life and wiggling with energy as she sought to sit still in "big people's" worship. Each of them was a unique and special child of God. All of them looked to the church to help them learn and grow in their faith.

In order to adequately educate these people and all the other children of God in our communities of faith, we must attend carefully to who they are. We need to see and understand them in all their many dimensions—biological, psychological, cultural, and theological. We need to take note of their own particular developmental journeys and find ways to nurture and support them. We need to offer them learning opportunities that meet their learning styles and make learning about their faith fun and enjoyable for them.

When I think of the "whos" we educate, I remember a verse and finger play I used to do with my children. It's probably familiar to many of you. "Here is the church. Here is the steeple. Open the door and see all the people." Attending to this essential building block of the participants in our educational ministries invites us to truly "see," to really notice *all* the people. In so doing, we will more faithfully assist them on their journeys in discipleship.

Reflection and Application

The following exercises are offered to assist readers in their engagement with the ideas presented in this chapter.

1. Review the four "perspectives on human beings" presented in this chapter. Consider the following:
    a. What new perspective would you add? What lens (or lenses) for looking at human beings is missing from this list? Why would you add this perspective?
    b. Rank the four perspectives, and any new ones you add, according to how well you believe your congregation pays attention to this perspective, number 1 being the perspective given the most attention in your church. (For example, if your church really pays attention to the biological needs of its members and gives thoughtful accommodation to them, the biological perspective would be number 1 on your list.)
    c. Review your rankings. What do you learn about your church and how it attends to its participants from this exercise?

2. Research what kind of information is requested when a person enrolls in a Sunday school class and/or

becomes a member of the church. (Some churches have cards or forms that persons fill out when they come forward on Sunday morning to present themselves for membership. Looking at these would be a good place to begin.) Do you think that this is important information to know? What additional information would be helpful for you to know about people? What does this exercise teach you about the ways in which your church pays attention to its members?

3. Review the material on perceptual learning styles presented in this chapter. Using this information, do the following:

   a. Analyze one or more lesson plans from the curriculum materials your church uses. Make a list of the perceptual learning styles used in these lessons (i.e., visual, print, haptic, etc.). Which styles seem to dominate? Which styles are missing? What steps might be taken to incorporate more of these sensory learning channels?

   b. Observe a Sunday school class in session. (Please make sure you have the teacher's and students' permission to do this!) What perceptual learning styles do you see engaged in this session? Which styles are missing? What might be done in this class to expand the styles used?

   c. Observe a worship service in your church. Make a list of the perceptual learning styles that are engaged during this service. What styles are missing? How might the worship service be changed to include more perceptual styles and open up learning for the participants?

4. What do each of these exercises teach you about how your church helps people learn? Discuss ways in which you might share your insights with the wider church.

Chapter 6

PROCESS AND METHOD:
How Do We Educate?

There is a knock at the door. It quietly opens to my invitation, "Come in." Standing in the doorway is a student with an anxious look on his face. "Can I talk with you for a moment?" he asks. I invite him to come in and ask him what I can do for him. The words come in a rush. He has to lead a youth retreat in a couple of weeks at his church, and he's never done this before. He needs some help. And then comes the question: "What do I do? Can you give me some help on what to do?"

I call this the "how to" question. The student is asking, How do I do this? It is the question that our last foundational building block for education in the church asks us to consider: How do we educate? It is a significant question to ask and calls us to pay attention to the processes and methods that we use to help people learn, but it is a question that needs to be approached with care. It is too easy to assume that if we just know how to do it, meaning that we know the right techniques and have learned the latest methods, our problems will be solved. The issue of how in educational ministry is more complex than that.

My response to the student's question, How do I do this? is the response I usually give when asked such a question: "It depends." I can see the immediate disappointment and frustration in his eyes. He was hoping I would tell him exactly what to do to guarantee a successful retreat and, instead, I respond, "It depends." But it does depend. It depends on our understanding of education and the purpose for which we are doing it (education for instruction may call for a different process than education for socialization). It depends on the context in which we are working, on the content we are teaching, and who the participants are. It also depends on the skills and abilities of the teacher or leader. All these will shape how we educate.

It is not easy to hear such an answer to the question about how to do it. We want easy solutions, but the church's educational ministry is a rich and multilayered endeavor and challenges us to wrestle with complex issues. It calls for our best efforts, and that means we need to approach the question of how to do it with the same careful attention that we have given to the other foundational building blocks discussed in this book. I would remind the reader once again that my goal here is not to provide a list of methods to use, but to engage in a thoughtful discussion of PROCESS and METHOD that offers insight for congregations as they seek to educate in their own particular settings.

Before going any further, I need to say something about the terms I use. You will note that I talk about both *process* and *method.* Often these terms are used to mean the same thing. But I want to distinguish them for our discussion here. I use *process* to refer to the broad approach we use in educating. A process is a series of actions that we take in order to accomplish our purpose. We may use a variety of methods within the process we choose, but the process provides us with the broad outline of how we will proceed. *Method* refers to those specific activities and techniques that we use to carry out the process. The focus of our discussion in this chapter will be on process. This comes from my own particular belief that there are many good resources available to provide us with methods to use.[1] What we need is an understanding of the process in order to have some criteria by which to select appropriate methods that will help us accomplish our educational tasks.

It is important to begin by sharing some basic assumptions that I make about process and method. These assumptions shape the discussion that follows. They also counter some of the misconceptions I often see at work in the church with regard to *how* we educate. Among my assumptions are:

1. *The process and methods do not educate or teach. People do!* The process we choose and the methods we use are simply tools to help us teach and learn. Rather than spending so much

time and so many resources in the church trying to find just the right approach or method, we need to give some attention to the people who are called to teach. They will be the ones who bring life to any process and method we choose. I am sure that there were others in Jesus' day who told stories and parables, but what people saw in Jesus was an incarnation of what he taught. It wasn't so much his process and method as it was his living presence that transformed the people around him. Attending to the skills and abilities of our teachers and helping them discover how they embody the truth of what they teach is an important part of how we educate.[2]

2. *The process and methods are shaped by the contexts within which they are used.* How we educate will depend on the particularity of a given situation. This assumption challenges the misconception that "one size fits all," or that one approach or method works equally well in all settings. A simple example is to think about working with visually challenged people. I am a visual person and like to use pictures, drawings, and writing on the board in my own teaching. But for people who cannot see, this approach is not helpful, and other methods must be found to engage them. When selecting a process and method to use, we have to give thought to the environment, to the people, and to the content in order to educate in ways that will truly connect.

3. *The process and methods should be consistent with the purpose toward which we educate.* How we educate should match why we are educating. In selecting a process and method we want to keep in mind the goal toward which we are striving. If we seek to educate people to be disciples of the Christ in the world today and to serve in continuity with Jesus' ministry of justice and mercy, our process and method must bear witness to this and truly help people to learn what that means. Relying on lectures, a traditional method in many adult church school classes, to help people learn what it means to serve seems to be a limited approach. An immersion experience with people engaged in actual service seems far more appropriate to help us reach our vision of discipleship. Our process and method need to fit our vision and help us educate for it.

4. *The tendency is to focus on method.* The emphasis in the church more often than not is on the methods that we use rather

than on the broader issue of the process that we will engage. We are enamored with technology in our culture and are easily caught up in the latest technique or gadget for doing something. We can see this with the growing use of computers in the church. Computers can be great teaching tools, but too often they are used as the latest method of choice without much thought being given to when and where they are appropriate and when not. A look at the broader question of process gives us the opportunity to consider the big picture and to know when a method fits and when it doesn't. To focus primarily on method is to be like a dancer focusing only on the individual steps rather than looking at the whole dance. Like the dancer, we forget where we are going, and the outcome is often stilted and disjointed.

5. *We tend to draw on a tried-and-true collection of familiar methods.* An old adage says that we teach as we are taught. We also teach to our own learning styles. We assume that this is the way to do it and continue with what is familiar and comfortable. However, this limits our ability to educate when the setting, the content, or the students call for another approach. Let me illustrate. The story of the healing of the bent-over woman found in Luke 13:10–17 is a story I have used on several occasions in various teaching situations. When I first started working with it, I would usually involve students in a discussion about the passage. I have a lot of experience leading discussions, and it is a very familiar method to me. But I realized that something was missing. Both the content of the story and the learning needs of the students called for something more than discussion. When I began to use role play and people were able to act out and embody the experience of being bent over, the insights gathered by the students took on new dimensions. Students were able to engage the story at a different level because of a different method. When I was able to move beyond my familiar collection of methods to engage in a new way, the education of my students was enhanced. The challenge is to expand our repertoire of methods in order to strengthen our educational work in the community of faith.

The assumptions that I have named may or may not be ones that you and your congregation make about process and method. What is important is that you give thought to and name the assumptions that do inform your approach to this important building block. Now, given my belief that the question of process is the more basic question to be addressed, let's turn our attention to a discussion of this important aspect of the "how to" building block for Christian education.

Process

When we consider how we are going to educate in the church, it is helpful to have a pattern, or what I call a process, in mind. Unlike the specific method we may use to teach a certain lesson or to lead a particular retreat, the process that we use is a broader approach, an informed, reflective manner of doing that provides us with a kind of blueprint for how we will go about our educational tasks.

Although there are a variety of processes that have been developed by various educators,[3] my purpose in looking at this matter is not to present a particular process as the one that should be used in all congregations. Instead, my goal here is to invite you to think about process and to consider the necessary qualities that need to be a part of whatever process is designed or selected.

What are the core qualities needed to shape the process or approach we use for educating in the church? I believe there are at least three. Our process needs to be (1) experiential, (2) reflective, and (3) relational.

1. Experiential

In many ways, to name *experiential* as a quality of the process that we use is to state the obvious, but we need to remind ourselves of the importance of experience in how we learn. Renate and Geoffrey Caine in their work on the brain and learning call our attention to this. They say, "One of the most important lessons to derive from the brain research is that, in a very important sense, *all* learning is experiential."[4] We need to be active participants in the processes used to help us learn.

The key here is not just the fact that our process of education needs to be experiential, but that we need to give thought to what kind of experiences they will be. As the noted philosopher of education John Dewey once said: "The belief that all genuine education comes about through experience does not mean that all experiences are genuinely or equally educative."[5] The Caines add support to this with insight from recent brain research: "Brain research establishes and confirms that multiple complex and concrete experiences are essential for meaningful learning and teaching."[6] It is not enough to say that we have experiential education when we simply place our adults in rows of chairs to listen to a lecture during church school. It is not enough to say that we have experiential education when we have young children gather in chairs around a table to hear a story and then to color some preprinted craft pages related to the story. As the Caines point out, the learner needs to be engaged in "talking, listening, reading, viewing, acting, and valuing."[7] And they need to be doing this in rich, multisensory ways.

When I think of experiential education in the church, I find myself reflecting on the model of Jesus as he taught his disciples. One particular encounter comes to mind, though there are many upon which we could reflect. The encounter is told in Mark 6:30–44, the familiar story about the feeding of the five thousand. When it came time for the crowds who had come to hear Jesus to find an evening meal, the disciples wanted to send them away to search for food. I imagine that the disciples wanted a break. They had been listening to Jesus for a long time and probably thought they had learned as much as they could for that day. But Jesus knew that their education in that moment was not complete. So he invited them into a "complex and concrete" learning experience. He told them, "You give them something to eat." You engage in the experience of feeding these people. In the moments that followed, I have a hunch that the disciples learned more than they could have imagined about what it meant to serve, about provision, and about the grace of God. This was experiential education at its best!

Whatever processes we choose for our educational work in the church, they need to be experiential in complex, rich, and multifaceted ways. Our call to be faithful in our forming of disciples challenges us to settle for nothing less.

2. Reflective

It is not enough that our educational process is rooted in experience. We also need to reflect on these experiences, to engage in the "active processing"[8] of them. We need time to think about and look at what we are doing. Our process for education in the church needs to include regular opportunity for reflection.

Again, this may seem like stating the obvious. Of course, reflection is a part of education, but I question how seriously we take this aspect of our "how to." When I think about my own educational experiences in the church, too many of my memories are of times when the church school hour or the Bible study session was filled with the presenting of the material with only a minute or two at the end left for discussion. Often that discussion was focused on whether we agreed or disagreed with what was said, and little time was spent in talking about why we thought the way we did or what difference any of it made in our daily living. I've been guilty of this as a teacher too. My focus can easily be on making sure I cover the material, and I end up leaving limited time for reflecting and making connections.

Reflection does take time. We need to see the reflective element of our process as more than just the "wait time" between our asking a question and the learner's responding. It calls for participation in a whole variety of questioning activities where we have the opportunity to ponder why we believe the way we do, where our beliefs came from, and what new ways of seeing and understanding may be needed for the future. Thomas Groome calls these activities "critical reasoning," "critical remembering," and "creative imagining," and they form the core of the reflective moment in his shared Christian praxis approach.[9]

Such reflection not only asks us to use our heads and our rational abilities, but also encourages the use of our hearts and our affective capacities. We need to help people name not only what they think, but what they feel. As Groome says, "Critical reflection is an affair of both the heart and the head."[10] We want Christians who not only think carefully about their beliefs, but who are also in touch with their feelings and are able to feel passionately about their faith and the world they are called to serve.

It is important to remember that reflection is not just a stage in a lesson. It does not occur at just one time, nor is it done in only one way. As the Caines suggest, "It is a matter of constantly 'working' and 'kneading' the ongoing experience that students have."[11] This reflective quality of our "how to" approach to Christian education calls us to take the time needed to truly engage and think about whatever it is we are learning. I am reminded of a friend of mine who shared an experience she had with a course that she was taking to complete a degree. When she received the reading list, she noted that there was only one book on it. This was certainly not typical of other courses she had taken, and she was curious. She discovered that they would indeed be reading only that one book during the semester. But they would be reading it *five* times. Her learning from that experience was the richness of insight one could find in a single book when there was time to continually reflect on it.

Whatever process we choose for carrying out education in the church, opportunities for ongoing reflection are basic to it. Only when we take the time for careful and patient reflection, when we realize that it isn't so much a matter of how much we cover but how well we come to know what it is we are studying, will we be faithfully engaged in the work of fashioning the people of God.

3. Relational

At its heart, education is a relational activity. Even those who claim that they are "self-educated" have had to relate to others through the books they have read and the experiences they have had. At issue here is not so much the fact that education is relational. Our concern sould be the quality and shape of those relationships.

We can relate to each other in a variety of ways. We can relate out of hierarchical, paternalistic models, where a few claim to know what is best and impose their attitudes and beliefs on others. We can relate as competitors, where the relationship is consumed with a need to prove who is right and who is wrong. We can relate as true friends, seeking the well-being of each other. We can relate as partners, committed to working alongside each other for a common goal.

My own belief is that not all relationships are equally good, nor are they equally appropriate for educational ministry. The question before us then is, What kind of relationships are appropriate for Christian education? Drawing on the root meaning of the term *education*, are there some models of relationship that more adequately address our call to "lead forth," to bring into reality that which is potential? Are there images of how people can relate that reflect the qualities we need in order to educate in faithful and meaningful ways in the church?

I believe that there are images for how we are to relate in our educational work in the community of faith. I want to name five kinds of relationships that exemplify the relational qualities appropriate for Christian education. Although certainly not an exhaustive list, these examples provide us with some clues to how we need to engage each other in teaching and learning. The images I want to highlight are partner, companion, midwife, sponsor, and guide.

A *partner* is a person who has a share or part with another. Partners work alongside one another, offering and receiving insight and help from one another. Partnerships are marked by mutuality, acceptance, and equal regard. When partnership becomes an image of how we do Christian education, we are called to take seriously our belief that all people are created in the image of God, that each of us is gifted and special in the sight of God, and that we need one another to accomplish God's work in the world. Children have things to teach the adults around them, and our youth have insights the church needs to hear.

As a community of faith, we are called to be partners, working together to build each other up in love, realizing that no one has all the answers. As teachers and educators, our students are not objects to be manipulated and shaped any way we like, as though we hold all the power. Instead, our students are "subjects with whom we enter into a relationship of mutuality and equality. Christian religious education is to be a subject-to-subject relationship of copartners."[12]

A *companion* is one who accompanies another. In our culture, a companion is often one who lives with, travels with, and assists another in a variety of ways. One of the stories that comes to mind when I think of how we are to be companions in our educational ministries is the story of Jesus and the two disciples on the road to Emmaus (Lk. 24:13–35). Here we have an image of companionship in the best sense of the term. Jesus was a companion to the two who found themselves bewildered and confused, returning to their homes not quite sure what had happened or what awaited them. He "companioned" them on this journey, providing assistance in helping each one to remember his own faith story and to see the events he had just experienced through the lens of this story. Jesus was truly *with* them in their journey. We are also called to be with those we educate in all the twists and turns of their lives.

It is interesting that the moment of clarity in this story came when Jesus broke bread with them. When we look at the root meaning of the word *companion,* we find that it comes from the Latin prefix *com,* which means "together," and *panis,* which means "bread." Companion literally means "one who eats bread with another." It is a powerful image for how we are to educate in the church. Whether we literally share bread or not, we are called to build relationships that truly feed one another and provide the sustenance we need for our journeys as disciples.

The image of *midwife* is another helpful one as we think about the relationships that will shape our educational processes in the church. A midwife is one who assists another in giving birth. However, "They know that their participation in the birthing process is limited to assisting something that can and will take place on its own and in its own time. The midwives not only exercise no control over the birthing process but also cannot even predict its outcome."[13] It is the same in our educational endeavors in the church. We are helping people give birth to their own vocations as children of God, but we cannot force it or make it happen within our time frame.

As midwives what we can do is help to create the best possible environment for this birth, a safe and hospitable environment where all is in readiness when the birth does occur. We can provide a stable presence for the one giving birth, helping the child, youth, or adult to focus on what is really needed at the moment. We can be a calming and trustworthy influence in the midst of the pain and effort required. In all our educational endeavors in the church, we need to relate in ways that help to bring to life the promises of God in all their abundance.

A *sponsor* is one who enables, whether it is through providing resources, offering encouragement, or making accessible what is needed. I think of people who sponsor young musicians or artists and provide the necessary resources and words of encouragement to help them develop their talent. The processes that we choose for educating in the church should to be shaped by this kind of relationship. We need to relate to our participants in ways that provide the resources necessary and make accessible the information and the experiences that will help them to grow in faith.

As sponsors, we are called to "encourage, make accessible the faith tradition, guide, and enable."[14] Bill Myers, in his book *Black and White Styles of Youth Ministry*, talks about an African American congregation that takes seriously its need to sponsor youth in their growth in faith. Their youth ministry is built on relationships with adults in the congregation who are committed to making accessible the African American cultural and faith traditions, which encourage and enable the youth to claim these identities as their own, and empower them to live these "unashamedly and unapologetically" in the world around them.[15] Such sponsoring relationships are needed in all congregations that take seriously the call to "make disciples."

A final image is that of *guide*. A guide is one who shows the way. Whereas partners, companions, midwives, and sponsors are important for our journeys in faith, there is also a need for those who can point the direction, show the way to go. We do this best when we go along with the people, pointing out the significant signposts, providing some commentary on what is happening and why, answering questions that arise, and giving shape and meaning to the journey. Just like a good tour guide, we help interpret and illuminate what people are seeing, hearing, feeling, and experiencing. Also, like a good guide, we are open to detours when the situation calls for it, and we welcome those spontaneous moments that cannot be planned, but offer rich and meaningful learning.

It is interesting that an old Teutonic word for "teacher" was the same word used for "index finger." Like an index finger, a good teacher is one who points the way, who indicates a particular direction, who calls our attention to something we have overlooked or have not yet noticed. We all need such guides in our lives, and Christian education that seeks to be faithful to its purpose will include relationships that guide us on our way.

How do we educate in the church? We educate through experience that is concrete and multisensory in rich and varied ways, through reflection that encourages us to move beyond the surface to explore the depths of our faith, and through relationships that invite us to be partner, companion, midwife, sponsor, and guide. Processes that are shaped by such experience, reflection, and relationships will lead to learning and growth.

Method

"What do I do?" The student's question that began this chapter continues to echo in our minds. More often than not, people asking this question are asking for a method to use. They want a specific technique or tool with which they can work in a given setting. My own approach, as modeled in this chapter, is to step back from the question of method to look at the issue of process and consider a broader perspective on how we educate. But this is not to discount the question of method. It is important to think about the specific means we will use to teach. A brief look at method and what we need to know about it seems in order now.

As previously mentioned, there are many resources available that provide lists and descriptions of methods.[16] My purpose here, then, is not to highlight particular methods, but to talk about some principles to guide our selection and use of various methods. What do we need to consider as we select the methods we will use in our educational ministries? Let me suggest some key guidelines for choosing methods. While certainly not an exhaustive list, these guidelines are, I believe, basic to the appropriate selection of the tools and techniques that we will use for educating in the church.

1. *Methods should be compatible with the content, the context, and the people in the educational setting.* When selecting methods to

use, we need to give attention to the content we are teaching, both what is being learned and how we want it to be learned. For example, when teaching about prayer, we want people to know how to pray, as well as to understand what prayer is. To rely simply on a lecture about prayer or some readings on prayer would be a limited choice of methods. To be compatible with our content and what we want to accomplish, interactive and participative methods that engage people in praying are needed.

We also need to attend to the context. When selecting methods, we need to think about the physical resources available to us and the kind of setting in which we are working. We are selecting an incompatible method when we choose to play a community-building game that requires a lot of movement and space and our church school class is located in a tiny room filled with tables and chairs. We need to either change our space or choose a more compatible method.

Knowledge of the people we seek to educate is critical when selecting methods. We need to understand the various learning styles present among our students. We need to pay attention to the physical limitations they have. For example, small children have difficulty with activities involving fine motor skills. They haven't yet developed these. When we decide to use an art project with them that contains many small pieces and requires a high level of finger and hand dexterity, we are not paying attention to the need for methods that match the students. Compatibility is an important guideline for choosing methods.

2. *The broader your repertoire of methods, the better.* A variety of methods is important. One of the key reasons for this has to do with the people we educate. As mentioned above, we need methods that are compatible with the people we educate. Since our participants come with many different learning styles, variety is essential in order to help engage the many styles.

Visual learners need to see pictures, illustrations, videos, displays, demonstrations, and have the opportunity to image while they are learning. Auditory learners need opportunities to listen and to verbalize. Using recordings, music, lectures, discussions, and other activities that involve hearing are important for these learners. Kinesthetic learners need to be physically engaged, participating in role plays and interactive games, using hands-on activities that involve their whole bodies in learning. With different learning styles and different abilities present in our congregations, variety truly becomes the spice of life, bringing energy and increasing the opportunity for learning to occur.

3. *It is important to think through and practice a new method before using it.* We need to have some familiarity with a method or technique before we use it. We need to have a sense of how the method works and how people might respond to it. Methods can take on a life of their own, and thinking through the possible responses and outcomes is important.

I become very aware of how a method can take on a life of its own when I use a technique like guided imagery. I remember using this method in a class on family ministry once. People were exploring their families of origin, and during the guided imagery experience, one of my students remembered an instance of abuse in her childhood. This had been a buried memory, and it was quite painful to call it to mind. Without some understanding of the method and knowledge of what might happen when used, I would have been unprepared to help the student and the rest of the class deal with this and come to some learning through it.

When exploring new methods, it is helpful to seek the advice and coaching of those experienced with the method. Participating in workshops where you can learn new methods and observe an experienced teacher or educator using such methods is an excellent way to add to your repertoire while gaining the knowledge and experience you need about how a method works.

4. *Remember that the purpose of a method is to help people learn.* It may seem that I am stating the obvious here. Of course, methods are to help people learn. Why else do we use them? Why, indeed. It is a good question and one that we need to explore. What purposes beyond helping people learn could influence our selection of a method?

Let me name three reasons I've seen at work in the selection of methods for teaching, purposes that can blind us to whether a method is appropriate for a particular educational setting. I believe that we sometimes choose methods (1) because "we've always done it that way," (2) in order to "look good," and (3) to duplicate an experience.

There are times when we use methods in the church because we are familiar with them, not because they help us teach in ways that our students can learn. We have simply always done it that way and have not stopped to ask whether it is really the best way to help our participants learn what they need to learn. There are times when we choose a method because it's the "groovy" thing to do. We want to look good, to be thought of as using the "latest" approach, even though the method we use does nothing to help the people in our particular setting learn. There are also times when we want to duplicate a particularly meaningful experience we have had and think that we can do this by using the exact same method. I see this happen with seminary students on a regular basis. They come to a particularly insightful learning through an experience in class and rush to duplicate it in their churches, generally to discover that it simply doesn't work that way. The setting, the people, the needs are not the same.

Doing something because it is familiar, because we are trying to impress, or because we want to duplicate an experience is not helpful for choosing the methods we use. The most important criterion for selecting a method is whether it helps the people with whom we work to learn.

Summary

The question of how we carry out the ministry of Christian education in the church is foundational to this important work. The processes that we use and the methods that we select need our careful and thoughtful attention. It is my hope that the discussion and guidelines offered in this chapter provide some helpful clues that assist the readers in making appropriate decisions and choices about how they will educate in their congregations.

Key to all of this, however, is the attitude that we carry into our work. Undergirding all our efforts to choose appropriate processes and methods should be an attitude of openness and flexibility. It is important to remember that the process by which we educate is not some rigid approach that we must follow in a lockstep and inflexible manner. This is not about finding the one right way. The process we use and the methods we choose are not fixed in concrete, never to be changed. Our approach to education in the church should be more like choreography, the designing of a dance, with rhythm and fluidity in what we do. We need to be able to improvise when the moment calls for it. The "how to" of Christian education is as much an artistic endeavor as it is a technological one. As Maria Harris observes, in this dance that we call Christian education, "There is no last moment (or final step). Instead, there is a continuing dance and a continuing rhythm."[17] May we be open to the One who asks us to dance and then leads the way.

Reflection and Application

The following exercises are offered to assist readers in their engagement with the ideas presented in this chapter.

1. Review the list of assumptions about process and method at the beginning of the chapter. Which of these have you seen at work in the church? What assumptions would you add to the list? After reading the chapter, what assumptions do you now want to make about how to educate in the church?

2. On a sheet of newsprint, make a list of the five relationship types—partner, companion, midwife, sponsor, and guide. Using this list, do the following:
   a. Recall an example from your own church experience when you have participated in any of these types of relationships. What was that experience like? In what ways was it beneficial to your growth in faith?
   b. From your experience, what images of relationship are missing from the list? Add these and describe

them. What do these types of relationships bring to the educational task?

c. What types of relationships seem to dominate in your church context? In what ways are these helpful? In what ways do they seem to inhibit learning?

d. What new relational qualities would you like to introduce in your educational ministry? How will you help this to happen?

3. On sheets of paper or newsprint, put the following headings: verbal methods, art methods, visuals, drama methods, music methods, paper and pencil methods, interactive methods. Under each heading, make a list of all the methods you have witnessed or experienced being used in educational ministry in your congregation. Then consider the following:

   a. Which category has the largest selection of methods? What kinds of methods seem to dominate? Which category has the fewest methods listed? Why do you think this is true? What could be done to expand the use of methods from that category?

   b. What new kinds of methods would you like to see introduced in your congregation? How might you accomplish this?

Chapter 7

ASSESSMENT AND EVALUATION:
How Are We Doing?

Although our foundation for Christian education is in place, we still need to consider some important aspects to this vital ministry. To continue with our imagery of laying a foundation, these aspects help to form the mortar that holds the building blocks together. In the final two chapters, I want to discuss two of these important aspects: (1) assessment and evaluation and (2) hindrances.

ASSESSMENT AND EVALUATION engage us with the question, How are we doing? It is an important question to ask on a regular basis. What's happening in our educational ministries? Are we accomplishing what we hoped to accomplish? How are things working? What needs to be changed? All of these are assessment and evaluation questions.

However, this is a process that we tend to overlook in the church. I think this has to do with some of our prior experiences with assessment and evaluation. Let me take you inside my classroom for just a moment. I've just asked the students to take out clean sheets of paper and put their names at the top. We are having a pop quiz. Immediately, I can feel the anxiety rise in the room. A test! The students are being assessed and evaluated. Apprehension is evident on their faces. I don't think their experience is unique. We all have memories of such moments when our hearts beat a little faster, our hands became sweaty, and we wondered how we would measure up.

Such memories color our understandings of assessment and evaluation. Many of our experiences with these processes carry negative connotations because we were told what was wrong with us, what we didn't know, and how we didn't measure up.

My experience in the church suggests that people tend to shy away from engaging in assessing and evaluating because of these memories. We want people to feel loved and accepted and don't want to engage in something that can cause hard feelings and lead to conflict.

Assessment and evaluation are not limited to pointing out what is wrong or how we failed. They also help us to see what is right and how we are succeeding. They can help us be better stewards of our resources and invest our time, energy, and finances in what helps us accomplish our educational goals in the community of faith. I believe that the strength and firmness of the foundation for Christian education that we have been building through the previous chapters is dependent on the ability to regularly assess and evaluate how we are doing. It is important mortar that helps to hold the foundation together.

Definition

What are assessment and evaluation? Are there ways of understanding these processes that help us to move beyond the negative memories and responses many of us have to these terms? Can we reclaim them as important aspects of our educational ministries in the church?

Although they are both a part of the same process, I understand them to be separate steps in that process. Assessment means to take the measure of something. It is a *descriptive* task that we do all the time, though often we do it without much conscious thought and in rather haphazard ways. When we assess an educational program or event, or assess the educational ministry as a whole by looking at the basics like purpose, context, content, participants, and so on, we are in essence taking a "measure"–finding out what happened, who these people are, what they are thinking and learning, what this setting is like.

Evaluation means to ascertain or fix value and worth. It refers to the ways in which we judge and place value on something. When we evaluate an educational program or event, we determine its value, whether it accomplished what we hoped it would, and if what it accomplished was valuable. In evaluation, we are naming not only what happened to people but also whether it was of value.

These two steps in the process seldom are done in isolation from each other. They are usually interconnected, with describing and evaluating occurring in close relationship with each other. While we are assessing a situation, we usually have some values in mind, something we've chosen as our "plumb line," that will be used to decide how well we think things are going. Evaluation is difficult to accomplish if we don't have some "data," some assessment on which to draw.

What is important to remember is that there is no "magic" to this process. In reality, we engage in it all the time! We take the measure of (assess) and make decisions regarding the value of (evaluate) things on a regular basis. We start new programs, eliminate old ones, change the format of a class, and so on, and we usually have some reasons for making those decisions. Too often, though, these decisions are made in the midst of crisis or on the spur of the moment without much conscious and careful thought. What is lacking is a focused intentionality about the process and how we come to make the decisions we do.

It is my belief that the more intentional we are in carrying out assessment and evaluation, the more the educational ministry of the church will benefit. I believe that we need to know both what is happening and how it is happening in our educational ministry. I believe that we need to ask questions about its value and be able to say whether it was good and of benefit to people's growth in faith and to the growth and faithfulness of the church.

Engaging in intentional assessment and evaluation on an ongoing basis helps the church to do several important things. It helps us (1) make decisions, (2) make changes, and (3) celebrate. By gathering the information we need and deciding what is of value to us, we are able to clarify the decisions we need to make in order to carry out our educational ministries in helpful and appropriate ways. Such clarity helps us then to decide, to actually make the needed decisions. Assessing and evaluating also provide us with the information we need to look carefully at what is and is not working, to acknowledge our failures and misguided adventures. The process helps us to see both our limits and our possibilities and provides us with the impetus to make the changes that are needed. Finally, assessment and evaluation help us to know and name our accomplishments, successes, and breakthroughs. The process helps us to celebrate, rejoice, and give thanks for the growing and deepening faith and witness to which our educational efforts have led.

Principles of Assessment and Evaluation

Like the foundational building blocks discussed in this book, the process of assessment and evaluation will be given its particular shape and form by the specific setting and nature of an individual congregation. However, there are some principles to guide our engagement in assessing and evaluating in our own particular contexts. Let me name five such principles.

1. *Do it in partnership.* It is important that our assessing and evaluating be a partnership effort and that everyone be involved in the process. This means that we do not have a few people gathering data and then making decisions about someone else's life, but that we invite those who are being assessed and evaluated to have a central role in the process. We do not do this *to* people, but *with* them.

Too often in the church, we do not include all the voices when we assess and evaluate a particular activity or ministry. This is particularly true when working with children and youth. I have been to many a Christian education committee meeting in which issues related to the children and youth were being discussed, but no one bothered to include them or their points of view in the assessment. Sometimes when their voices are included, they are discounted with comments like "They are too young to know what they think" or "They don't really care." A not-so-subtle paternalistic attitude of "We really know best" can prevail in such situations, and the opportunity to truly take the measure of the situation, to know how those involved feel, to understand what is of value and importance to them, is lost.

I am fully aware that working in partnership takes time. There is a certain inefficiency in having to consult various people and listen to different points of view and try to find some consensus out of it all. It can slow the effort down and lead to a longer decision-making process. But such a commitment to engaging all voices seems to me to be most faithful to a God who calls us to make room at the table for everyone.

2. *Use a variety of approaches.*[1] We need to engage a variety of approaches in our assessment and evaluation process. To use only a paper and pencil approach, like printed surveys to gather information about a congregation or a printed evaluation form to garner people's responses at the end of a class or event, will limit the data we have available for making our decisions. Such forms shape people's responses by the questions that are asked and the options that are presented. This is not to say that such forms are not helpful and should not be used; it is to point out that they offer limited information.

For broader and more complete information, it is important that we also engage in actual conversations with people,[2] talking with them one-on-one as well as in groups and giving them the freedom to say what they want and respond in ways appropriate for them. When I ask students to evaluate courses, I use both a printed evaluation form and an oral process. The students gather in small groups and talk among themselves about how the course was and was not helpful. A recorder for each group records all the responses, and these become a part of the assessment and evaluation data.

We need to make sure that such situations are "safe," that people feel free to be open and honest, that they know who will receive the information they provide and how it will be used. This is true of any approach we use. People need to be informed about why they are being asked for information and in what ways it will be used.

Observation is also a helpful approach. Sometimes an outside observer can provide insight that is very useful in a situation. I have found this to be particularly helpful when a church finds itself in a place of conflict and seems in a quandary about what to do. An outside observer's assessment of the situation can provide an important perspective and help a church move through the impasse. I also know of church school teachers having difficulty with a class who invite an experienced teacher to sit in and observe. These observations often provide a new way of seeing and may suggest the solution to the problem.

The use of videotaping to help teachers assess themselves can be very helpful. I do not believe that people should ever be coerced into this, but I do know of church school teachers who find the opportunity to see themselves in action to be a powerful assessment and evaluation tool for their own teaching practice. Any approach that helps people take a look at themselves and their own practices can be useful in assessing and evaluating educational ministry.

Perhaps as important as the approaches we use is conveying the attitude that assessment and evaluation are important. It is not about finding faults but about helping people grow. We also need to let people know that what they have to say is significant to us. I think of the number of times I've completed an evaluation form and wondered if it really mattered at all. One of the ways we convey that others' perspectives matter is to let them see the difference it makes. When I ask students to evaluate a course, I point out to them both the changes I've made and the things I do the same as a result of previous student evaluations. We all need to know that our input matters.

3. *The "thicker" the information we have, the greater the possibility that our assessment and evaluation will be appropriate and helpful.* What this principle means is that we need to assess and evaluate from a variety of perspectives, through multiple lenses, to gather as much information as possible. The previous principle regarding the use of a variety of approaches helps us collect this thick information. Each tool we use can help us uncover some new information or a different way of viewing the situation.

What do we mean by "thick" information? Let's take an example. If we want to evaluate the church's ministry with children, we need to gather information from the children themselves, from the parents and other family members, from teachers, and from others in the congregation who have contact with the children. We need to know something about child development and how children learn, grow, and develop in faith. We need to look at the resources we have for working with children, both in the church and in the wider community. We need to note what we are already doing and how that is working. We need to determine what children need from our ministry. Each piece of information adds another layer to our description and helps us by providing the kind of rich, thick picture we want in order to determine how we are doing in our ministry with children and how we might need to change.

Such a thick description is helpful throughout our assessing and evaluating. It enables us to really know a situation and to have as full and adequate a measure as possible. It helps us to see what we truly value and also opens options that we might not have seen with a more superficial look at the issue before us. Taking the time to develop an in-depth description is well worth the effort.

4. *Share the findings.* After we have completed the assessment and evaluation process, we need to share what we discovered and decided with others. We need to let people know what we learned. Those involved with a particular program or ministry especially need to know what is going on and why. To keep the information in the hands of a few leads to an imbalance of power, causing people to feel they are just objects being manipulated by others.

I believe that this is the seat of some of the resistance to change that we experience in the church. People see things happening, but they don't know why. No one has shared with them the process by which these decisions were made. They don't know what information was used to make the decision or the criteria upon which the decision was based. The more open and honest we are in sharing the findings of our assessment and evaluation, the greater the likelihood that such resistance will be avoided and the needed changes will result.

5. *Keep it in perspective.* There are two ways in which we need to keep our assessment and evaluation in perspective. First, we must not fall into the trap that assessment and evaluation will guarantee us a successful educational ministry. We may constantly assess and evaluate, but if we aren't committed to actually carrying through on the findings of this process and making the needed changes, little will come from our efforts.

We see this happen regularly in our society. Be it government, business, public schools, or other societal institutions, a special task force is named to "study" a situation, in other words, to assess and evaluate it. The reports of these task forces are presented, sometimes with a great deal of fanfare, and then nothing happens. The same is true in the church. We study a situation, determine what is of value, know what needs to be done, and then seem to lack the will to do it. Our efforts at assessment and evaluation are only as good as our willingness to take action with the outcomes.

Finally, we need to maintain the perspective that assessment and evaluation are *not* about failure and punishment. Their purpose is not to make us feel guilty or berate ourselves about how bad we are at something. The purpose of assessing and evaluating is to help us to see clearly. As Elliot Eisner says, "Seeing is central to making."[3] In order to build a strong and faithful educational ministry, we need to be able to see clearly. Seeing clearly calls us to pay attention to what is happening and how it is happening, to discover where growth and change are possible, and to celebrate the gifts we have to offer. We undertake this important process of assessment and evaluation in educational ministry in order to be faithful to our call to "make disciples." What we ultimately seek is knowledge that will help us to more faithfully fashion the people of God.

Establishing a Plumb Line

A remaining question to be addressed in this discussion of assessment and evaluation has to do with what criteria we will use to determine the value of our educational efforts. How will we judge our work and determine if it has been successful or not? Like God setting a plumb line in the midst of the Israelites (Am. 7:7–8), we need to set in our midst criteria by which we are going to evaluate whether we've accomplished what is appropriate and faithful to the gospel call.

Let me say again that my purpose here is not to name the criteria that the church should use. Each congregation needs to think through this issue for itself. Because it invites the church to think through why it is educating, the material on purpose in chapter 2 can be very helpful in this process. The purposes and goals we have for educational ministry give us a vision toward which we are moving, and it seems appropriate to measure our efforts in light of how they help us meet these.

Let's look at some examples of how purpose is suggestive of a plumb line. The Search Institute's study of Christian education, mentioned earlier, claims that the primary aim of congregational life and therefore Christian education is "to nurture...a vibrant, life-changing faith, the kind of faith that shapes one's way of being, thinking, and acting."[4] Such a purpose offers us criteria for evaluation and encourages us to ask the question, How well are we helping to nurture a life-changing faith, an integrated faith involving both a life-changing relationship with God and a commitment to serving others? When Thomas Groome says that "the purpose of Christian religious education is to enable people to live as Christians, that is, to live lives of Christian faith,"[5] he is also offering criteria for evaluating a congregation's educational efforts. The evaluation question becomes, In what ways and how well are we helping people to live their Christian faith in their daily experiences? This becomes a plumb line to help us decide if our education is accomplishing what we hoped. When I talk about continuity and change as a broad purpose for Christian education, I, too, am offering a criterion for evaluation. Here the question becomes, How well do our educational efforts help us stay rooted in the story, vision, and tradition (continuity) and also lead us to transformation, liberation, and changed lives and societies (change)?

Clearly, scripture offers us some "plumb lines" worthy of our attention as we undertake to assess and evaluate our educational work. Micah 6:8 talks about what is required of us and lists three tasks: Do justice, love kindness, and walk humbly with God. The evaluation question for the community of faith becomes, How adequately does our education help people learn to do justice, love kindness, and walk humbly with God? In Matthew 22:37–39, Jesus names the great commandment, a plumb line for all Christians: "'You shall love the Lord your God with all your heart, and with all your soul, and with all your mind.' This is the greatest and first commandment. And a second is like it: 'You shall love your neighbor as yourself.'" The question we then ask of our educational efforts is, How well do we help people learn to keep these commandments? A final (though this list is certainly not exhaustive) example of the "plumb lines" that scripture offers can be found in Matthew 25:31–46, the story of the last judgment. Here we are called to feed the hungry, give drink to the thirsty, welcome the stranger, give clothing to the naked, care for the sick, and visit those in prison. Clearly, the evaluation question that would be asked is, How well have we helped people to respond to and live this vision of discipleship?

Whatever plumb line we choose, having one is central to the assessment and evaluation process. Through conversation and study in the church we need to work together to name our purpose and goal, to identify our plumb line, and then to use this to evaluate how we are doing in our educational ministries. The importance of what we are about calls for nothing less.

Summary

Assessment and evaluation is not a new process in our lives. Throughout our daily experience we are constantly, albeit often subconsciously, taking the measure of people and situations around us and deciding what we value. We are also doing this in the church. Seldom do we participate in any event, be it worship, fellowship, church school, or whatever, that we do not take some note of what is happening and whether we like it or not.

My call here to take seriously assessing and evaluating in the church is not a call to something new. Instead, it is a call to be intentional and deliberate about the process, to regularly ask the question, How are we doing? and to take the time to find out. It is a call to include as many voices as possible in the conversation, to use different tools and perspectives to gather our information, to create a rich and broad picture of what is happening, to keep the congregation regularly informed as to what we are discovering, and to always keep our perspective on what we are doing. It is finally a call to name the plumb line we will use to hold ourselves accountable for the work we do in educating, in leading people forth into their vocations as disciples of Christ.

Reflection and Application

The following exercises are offered to assist readers in their engagement with the ideas presented in this chapter.

1. Think about your own experiences with assessment and evaluation. How did these make you feel? What is your general response to being assessed and evaluated? How do you think this influences your understanding of assessment and evaluation in the church? What new perspectives on this process have you gained from reading this chapter?

2. Name some of your own experiences with assessment and evaluation in church settings. How was it done? How did you feel about it? What were the results or outcomes from it?

3. Brainstorm a list of all the approaches you can think of by which assessment and evaluation are and can be done in the church setting. Indicate which of these you have actually experienced. Which ones have you found most helpful? What approach would you like to see your own church use that it currently does not? Why do you think this approach would be helpful in your context?

4. Choose one of the three scriptures mentioned as providing a plumb line for evaluating an educational ministry: Micah 6:8, Matthew 22:34–39, or Matthew 25:31–46. Read the scripture and consider the following questions:
    a. What are the marks of being a Christian that are expressed here? State these in your own words.
    b. In what ways would you be able to identify these qualities in a person's life? What would tell you that they were living and embodying that image?
    c. How would this scripture help your church evaluate its educational ministry?

5. Make a list of other scriptures that you believe are suggestive of a plumb line to be used for evaluating the church's educational efforts.

Chapter 8

HINDRANCES:
What Stands in Our Way?

"We've never done it that way before." How often have you heard these words echo through the halls of your church? Although they could be simple words of description, pointing to the fact that something new is being tried, often they are words that hinder, blocking what is new and seeking to maintain the status quo.

"We've never thought about these things before," or "We already know all that." Either of these could be the response to the discussion about the building blocks of Christian education in the previous pages. Again, they might be a simple description of reality, but there is also the possibility that they reflect a resistance to considering something that could lead to change. "Why do we need to think about these 'building blocks' of Christian education? We know what we are doing. We've been doing it for years."

There is something in the nature of human beings and of institutions that resists change. It is natural for us to be drawn to that which is familiar, that which is tried and true. Yet at its core, education is about change. As already noted, the very word itself comes from a Latin word that means to lead forth, to move from the familiar into the unknown. It simply doesn't make sense to say that we have been educated, but we haven't changed.

Yet we seem to resist change. Both knowingly and unknowingly, we block important changes that need to be made. We hinder important discussions that need to be held. We avoid looking at ideas that challenge us and call us to respond.

We aren't the first in the Christian community to face what I call HINDRANCES. Even our ancestors in the faith had to struggle with hindrances to their growth as disciples. In Romans 7:15 the apostle Paul gives eloquent voice to his struggles. He says, "I do not understand my own actions. For I do not do what I want, but I do the very thing I hate." There was that within Paul that hindered him in his Christian journey. Peter, in his encounter with Cornelius as told in Acts 10, had to face beliefs that hindered him from receiving Cornelius into the Christian community. To return again to Jesus' temptation in the wilderness, I believe that this is a story of hindrances, of Jesus' coming face-to-face with that which could stand in the way of his mission and ministry. He had to face squarely each of these potential hindrances to claim with clarity the path his journey would take.

And so it is with us. If we want to take seriously our call to educate in the Christian community, we need to give attention to those things—actions, attitudes, emotions, values, assumptions, beliefs, and so on—that can hinder our work. We need to look at what can stand in our way, what might prevent us from moving Christian education to center stage and renewing this vital ministry. Unless addressed, hindrances will weaken the mortar that holds our foundation together.

Like things that go bump in the night, hindrances are more powerful, frightening, and effective when they are ignored and not named. They become much less powerful when we turn on the light, look at them clearly, and name them for what they are. This doesn't mean that the hindrances will go away. Our promise is not of an unhindered path. Instead, naming the hindrances helps free us to decide how we might go through, work around, or chart a new course to carry out the work of educational ministry.

This chapter names some of the hindrances that I have seen at work in the church. The list is not meant to be an exhaustive one, and I encourage you to give thought to those hindrances that you experience in your own setting. I offer this list as a means of highlighting what might work against us in our educational efforts in the hope that it will shed some light for you too.

Hindrances

Fear

"The only thing we have to fear is fear itself." This famous quote from Franklin Roosevelt names the first hindrance we often face as we consider an important issue, develop a new idea or approach, or try something different in the church. Fear is a natural and useful human emotion, but it can also be what Carlos Castañeda calls an "enemy of learning."[1] It causes us to retreat, to draw back, to stop searching and questioning, to stop wanting to know and understand.

We seem to live with fear a lot in our world today. As Henri Nouwen said, "We are a fearful people...The agenda of our world—the issues and items that fill newspapers and newscasts—is an agenda of fear and power."[2] Many people do not like to associate fear with the church. Church is one place where one should feel safe and secure. We think that fear is not an appropriate emotion for the church setting and often avoid acknowledging its presence. Yet even in the community of faith, fear is a reality.

When we face something new, a change in a familiar pattern or way of doing things, or when we come up against a challenge to a cherished belief and find that other people see it differently, our response is often fear. We can experience it as a low-level sense of anxiety or as a heart-pounding sense of impending danger. Whichever way, we feel out of control and search for a way to respond.

The responses to fear take many forms. Sometimes we run away from the change and fall back into the tried and familiar. For example, instead of trying the new Bible study materials that challenge some of our perspectives, we continue with materials that we have used for many years. Another response is to become rigid in our thinking, allowing no doubts or questions to be raised. The comment here is "That's just the way things are. We are to accept them, not raise questions." Sometimes we escape into what I call relativism, where we don't really commit ourselves to anything. We say that one way is as good as another and continue to muddle along.

I see fear as a factor in the response of the religious leaders of Jesus' day to his ministry. I do not believe that the Pharisees and Sadducees were "bad" people. I do not think that they intended evil things. Instead, I think that they were afraid of the challenges and changes Jesus brought and that their response was to become even more rigid in their thinking and to hold fast to the tried and familiar ways of doing things.

Fear *is* an enemy of education. It causes us to draw back, to stop seeking, to stop wanting to know. It hinders our ability to be open, to look carefully and critically at alternative perspectives, and to change in appropriate ways. It inhibits our willingness to explore new thinking and welcome diversity.

However, let me speak a word of caution here. The reason for facing a fear is not to remove it from our midst so that we are open to anything and everything. The fears we experience can legitimately be telling us to proceed with care and caution, that we are dealing with important things, and that we need to be careful. The reason we face our fear is so that the fear does not control us, that it is not the determining factor in what we decide to do.

I am a fan of the old television series *M*A*S*H*. As I remember it, there was an episode where Colonel Sherman Potter, the doctor in charge of the unit, operated on a young soldier. He forgot to remove one of the sponges used in the surgery, and the young man developed an infection. Hawkeye, one of the other doctors, had to operate again to remove it. Colonel Potter was quite shaken by the incident, knowing that the young man could have died from the infection.

Potter's response to this was to withdraw into himself. He was cross in his interactions with others and refused to perform any operations. The members of the unit knew that something was wrong but didn't know how to respond. They found a way to bring to their camp an army psychiatrist, Sidney, to check on Potter. In their conversation, Potter told Sidney about the incident and his concern. He was filled with fear that he was getting old, too old and forgetful to be operating anymore. Sidney was honest and said that there would come a day when Potter would need to stop. However, knowing the control that the fear had on Potter's current behavior, Sidney continued with a very powerful statement. He said, "But Sherman, don't let the fear make the decision for you."

It is when our fears become the controlling factor in our decisions and we decide on the basis of feeling afraid that fear becomes a true hindrance in our lives. I see this happen in the church time and again. We explore a new approach to something but discover that it raises feelings of fear and anxiety. People resist and respond with comments such as "We've never done it this way before." And so we retreat and decide not to continue with the new idea. Sometimes we decide not to even try something new because of our fear of the reactions we might face. We make our decision on the basis of the fear that we experience or anticipate.

As with all the hindrances we will discuss, I want to propose an alternative way. Instead of retreating because of our fears, we need to look them fully in the face. We need to name what they are and look at what they are trying to tell us. Are we moving too fast without helping people understand what we are doing? Then we need to take time to help people understand. Have we discarded all that is familiar so that people have no sense of security as we venture into new areas? We need a balance of the familiar and the new in our ventures. Have we provided ways for people to voice their fears so they do not bear them in silence? Often it is what we haven't been able to say that holds the most power over us.

The challenge is to move from fear to courage, to transform our fears into the courage to risk, to change, and to be open to God's spirit, moving in new and transforming ways in our midst. When we move from fear to courage, we discover the strength to move forward. In the garden of Gethsemane, Jesus faced his fears and moved from fear to the courage to set his face to the journey before him. As his followers, we are called to do likewise.

False Clarity

This hindrance may seem a bit confusing at first. After all, one would think that clarity is our goal in education. We want to see and think clearly. A word of explanation is needed. *False* clarity refers to the mind-set that thinks we have the answer. "My mind's made up. I know what to think. Don't confuse me with anything else!"

What happens with false clarity of mind is that we become blind to that which is around us. As Castañeda puts it, "It forces the man[*sic*] never to doubt himself. It gives him the assurance he can do anything he pleases, for he sees clearly into everything."[3] This leads to the arrogant assumption that we have the "right" answer and that our task is to see that others accept that answer too. We want them to be as "clear" as we are.

We see this kind of clarity at work in the world today in the rising tide of fundamentalism affecting many of the world's religious communities. Those who claim to have the "fundamentals" operate out of a sense of clarity that says that they are right and everyone else is wrong. Any who choose to question, doubt, or raise another perspective are accused of false belief and are excluded from the community.

The danger for education is that we stop learning. If we already know the truth, if we are already clear about it, we don't need to bother with more knowledge or information. We take what Paulo Freire calls a "banking" approach to education.[4] Our task is simply to "deposit" our clarity in others, and they will be just fine. There is no longer room for doubts and questions, for alternative perspectives through which God might speak a new word to us.

I have a lot of sympathy for the apostle Thomas. He was openly honest about his doubts and would not accept something simply on the word of another. He wanted to see and experience for himself. Jesus obviously took Thomas seriously too. When he appeared to the disciples, he did not chide Thomas for his doubts. He did not say, "Why do you doubt?" Instead, he invited Thomas to see for himself: "Put your finger here and see my hands. Reach out your hand and put it in my side. Do not doubt but believe" (Jn. 20:27). It was only after Thomas was able to see and experience that Jesus called him to doubt no longer. We all need moments when we claim our doubts and questions and go in search to see and experience for ourselves on this journey of faith. Someone else's clarity simply won't do.

However, another word of caution needs to be spoken. The opposite of false clarity is not a life based only on questions, doubts, and relativism. The answer to false clarity is not an attitude that "anything goes." It is important to make commitments, to claim our beliefs, to set our hearts on that which matters to us, and to live faithfully in response to it. The opposite of false clarity is not a mindless relativism. Instead, it is a thoughtful commitment to give attention to what we believe and being willing to embrace doubt and questions as pathways into deeper understanding. We pay heed to Rainer Maria Rilke's advice to his young friend:

> Be patient towards all that is unsolved in your heart and try to love the questions themselves like locked rooms...Do not now seek the answers; that cannot be given you because you would not be able to live them. And the point is, to live everything. Live the questions now. Perhaps you will then gradually, without noticing it, live along some distant day into the answer.[5]

False clarity hinders our work of renewing and transforming educational ministry in the church. False clarity is at work when we refuse to look at curriculum materials and resources from a variety of places, insisting instead that only one source of materials is the correct and appropriate one for a church's use. False clarity is at work when we insist that there is only one right way to structure a church school (for example, along age-segregated lines) or only one translation of the Bible that can be used in Bible study.

My hope is that we can move beyond false clarity to a thoughtful openness that allows us to raise our doubts and questions and invites us to explore alternatives and consider new possibilities for educational ministries in our local settings. If we find ourselves operating out of false clarity, thinking that we know exactly how something should be done and resisting any other viewpoints, it is time to pause and say, "But what if...?" What if we tried this? What if we looked at it from this perspective? What if we considered this possibility? "What if" allows space for dreaming dreams and naming visions. Into such space God can bring new life!

Presumptions

Another hindrance that blocks our work of empowering and transforming Christian education is one I call *presumptions*. Presumptions are those preconceived notions, the taken-for-granted ideas that we have about people and things. We all have them, and some presumptions actually help us move more smoothly through the day. We presume, take for granted, that the sun will come up in the morning and go down in the evening. We presume that when we turn on a faucet, clean water will emerge from it. We presume that most people will obey the traffic laws as we drive to work. We presume these things every day, and in our taking them for granted we do not have to give them much thought. Our attention and energy can be given to other things.

Presumptions become a problem when they create blind spots. When we take something for granted, we stop seeing it, paying attention to it, and therefore miss changes that occur that give us cause to alter how we respond. I am told that counterfeit artists can disguise a one-dollar bill as a twenty and people will accept it. When they see the number 20 on the bill, they presume that it is correct, never really looking closer at other details.

Presumptions are present in the church and create blind spots that hinder our visioning of new things. I saw some presumptions at work in the research I did on church school teachers for my doctoral dissertation.[6] Many of the teachers presumed that the school model (children in a classroom sitting in chairs around a table) was the way they had to teach. They presumed that the children learned the same way that they, the teachers, did, so they used the methods they liked and from which they had learned. They presumed that since this was a volunteer job and only took forty-five minutes to an hour on Sunday morning, they didn't need to put much time into it. They presumed that the church really didn't care what they were doing as long as they were there each Sunday, so they tended to teach what they thought was important, no matter what the curriculum materials presented.

I don't mean to paint a negative picture of these teachers. They were very dedicated and caring people. But they did much of their teaching on the basis of presumptions. They simply took for granted certain perspectives and ways of doing things and never gave it much thought. And it is to the church's discredit that it seldom invited them to do such thinking!

When we presume that Sunday school is the only setting for Christian education, when we presume that age-segregated classes are the only way to teach, when we presume that people learn only in certain ways, when we presume that we can't ask much of our church school teachers because they are only volunteers, when we make any of a long list of presumptions about educational ministry in the local church, we have created a hindrance to the kind of creative thinking and analysis needed for renewing and transforming Christian education. We stop looking for other viewpoints, other possibilities, and other approaches.

What is needed is a movement from presumption to paying attention. My husband has often shared with me the story of one of his seminary professors, whose favorite word was *observation.* When his students seemed to be overlooking critical facts or information, this professor would challenge them by saying, "Observation!" He called them to look and see, to notice what was before them.

Daniel Aleshire talks about the importance of paying attention in his book *Faithcare.* He believes that paying attention "provides the information required for articulate expressions of ministry."[7] It is "crucial for the ongoing education and program ministry of the congregation"[8] and "requires us 'to look' and 'to see'—with an awareness of our focus, a sensitivity to our vision, and proper use of lenses that clarify our perception."[9]

When we stop presuming and take the time to look and see, we will notice that people learn in many different ways. We will notice that Christian education takes place in a variety of settings. We will notice that old and young people share common concerns and can learn together and from each other. When we stop presuming, we will be able "to pay attention to the people who question and celebrate, grieve and believe, and to envision expressions of ministry that help them learn the lessons of faith and grow to maturity as faithful people."[10]

Routine

A fourth hindrance is one I name *routine.* I remember a song I used to sing as a very little child. I think it was a way to help me learn the days of the week. It went something like this: "This is the way we wash our clothes, wash our clothes, wash our clothes. This is the way we wash our clothes, all on a Monday morning." There was a different activity for every day of the week. I don't remember them all, but I remember, "iron our clothes, all on a Wednesday morning" and "go to church, all on a Sunday morning." What I also remember is that this song described the routine of daily life in my childhood home. My mother generally washed on Monday, ironed on Wednesday, cleaned on Friday, and we all went to church on Sunday. It was the established pattern of our existence. In fact, it took some time and effort in my own adult life before I could vary from this routine without feeling a little guilty, that I was somehow not quite doing it right!

Routine is a reality of life. Most of us have our customary and regular ways of doing things. Like the presumptions we make, routines can assist us in our lives, provide us with some pattern and order that frees energy for other activities. However, routine becomes a hindrance when we follow these customary patterns in a rote, mindless, and unvarying manner. To limit washing to Mondays or ironing to Wednesdays without giving thought to other possibilities is to allow routine to hinder our lives.

Those words you have heard mentioned several times in these pages, "We've always done it this way," often signal a routine that has become entrenched and is now a rigid status quo: "We've always selected church school teachers in this way"; "We've always held our vacation church school at that time"; or "We've always done the Christmas pageant this way."

What happens when routine becomes rote and unvarying is that we stop seeing the possibilities that are before us. My husband and I are walkers. We usually begin our day with a two-mile walk. Being a person who likes routine, I like to pick a route and stick to it. Brent, however, likes variety and is always suggesting a new path to take. What I have discovered is that his invitation to step out of the routine and try a different route enables me to see things I might not otherwise see. His invitation to diversity provides me with new vistas and new experiences that enrich my life.

I suggest that the same is true in the church. When we are willing to move beyond routines that hinder and bind us, when we are willing to embrace diversity and welcome other ways of doing things, we are often blessed with new insights and the experience of a God who is waiting to surprise us in rich and exciting ways.

The Tyranny of the Urgent

The *tyranny of the urgent* is another hindrance at work in the church. We live in a day of the "instant": instant coffee, instant communication, instant pain relief. It seems that if it doesn't happen *now*, it is of no use to us. We want a pill that will work *now*. We want to solve whatever problem is facing us *now*. We lurch from urgency to urgency in our culture, from the current crisis to the next one. News is considered "old" after a matter of a few hours. I sometimes think that we even go looking for the urgent, looking for the next crisis that will excite us and get the adrenaline going. I think we are a culture addicted to the urgent.

The church is not immune to this tyranny of the urgent. We want to fix our problems *now*. If we try something new and it doesn't work the way we hope *right away*, our response is often to scrap whatever it is and move on to the next new idea. Because it doesn't work right now, it must not be the right thing. We don't take the time to analyze what happened, to look at the complex nature of change and how it happens. Instead we want the quick fix and urgently move on to trying something else.

The problem with all this is that it ignores reality. Change does not often happen overnight. It takes time and patience. Many of the issues facing the church have been a long time in the making and do not lend themselves to immediate solutions. We have to realize that we are in this for the long haul. When people ask me how I keep working at issues of educational ministry in the church when there are so many discouraging signs with regard to this endeavor, I tell them I am doing this for my grandchildren and great-grandchildren. I may not see the results, but the future of the church calls for our long-term commitment. Like water consistently and steadily dropping on a rock, if we patiently persist, the channel for a great river will eventually emerge.

The challenge here is to move from this tyranny of the urgent to what I call *radical patience*, a patience that knows that change, like life itself, takes time. As Sue Bender in her book *Plain and Simple*, the story of her sojourn with the Amish, says, "Miracles come after a lot of hard work."[11] When we feel the pressure of the urgent in the midst of church life, we can place our trust in that steadfast, eternal love that demonstrates a radical patience beyond anything we can imagine, and know that we have all the time we need.

The "Messiness" of Life

The final hindrance I want to mention is one I call the *messiness* of life. I give credit to my faculty colleague Dr. Peggy Way for introducing me to this term. Messiness points to the reality that life is not simple, neat, and predictable. Things happen that we did not plan; people do not respond in the way that we had hoped; and we realize that we are not as much in control as we had thought.

The hindrance in this instance is not so much the fact that life is "messy," but is the way that we respond to this messiness. We deny it, try to avoid it, or try to "fix" it. We live under the illusion that there is the perfect life out there, that "Truth" with a capital T is just around the corner, and that if we just do it "right," our problems will be solved. Life will be under control, and we will have a successful educational ministry.

I hear this in students who want me to give them simple answers to how to do educational ministry. I hear it in pastors, ministers of Christian education, and concerned laity who want the program or resources that will solve their problems. I see the denial of the messiness of life at work when the church tries new curriculum materials and some of the teachers complain. Or they select a new time for Bible study and fewer people than anticipated take part. All too often the church's response is to drop the new materials or give up on the new time. Energy is not given to analyzing what is happening, to looking at the complex nature of change and how change takes place. Instead, we continue to look for the easy solution to our problem that we just know is out there. We only have to find it.

The difficulty with all this is that it ignores reality. The church is a complex setting where people with different points of view are asked to work together, where tensions and ambiguities are a part of daily life, and where problems often do not lend themselves to simple solutions. Change takes time and is generally not a simple process. What works in one place will not work in another, no matter how hard we may try.

The reality is that there is no perfect program, no perfect approach, no one right way of doing it. There are useful and helpful approaches, programs, and ways of doing things that may be applicable in a given setting at a given time; but we kid ourselves if we think that we can find the way to solve the issues facing Christian education once and for all. The discussion we've been having in this book is a discussion we need to visit again and again. It needs to be an ongoing dialogue whose purpose is to keep us open and aware, alert to the changes and complexities in our situation, and able to make appropriate choices and decisions as the need arises.

Our challenge is to move from denying, avoiding, or trying to "fix" the messiness of life around us to embracing the complexities and ambiguities and paying attention to what they may have to teach us. It is often in the unplanned and unexpected that we meet the God who loves and cares for this messy, broken, human world in ways far beyond our comprehension. We can place our trust in that steadfast, eternal love and move forward to embrace the challenges before us, knowing that we are not called to do it "right" but to live faithfully the journey that is ours.

Summary

One of the best-loved stories of Jesus is about his encounter with children. Mark tells it this way:

> People were bringing little children to him in order that he might touch them; and the disciples spoke sternly to them. But when Jesus saw this, he was indignant and

said to them, "Let the little children come to me; do not stop them; for it is to such as these that the kingdom of God belongs. Truly I tell you, whoever does not receive the kingdom of God as a little child will never enter it." And he took them up in his arms, laid his hands on them, and blessed them. (Mk. 10:13–16)

In the *Revised Standard Version of the Bible*, the phrase "do not stop them" is translated "do not hinder them." Jesus challenged his disciples to look carefully at the ways in which they were hindering the very least of those whom he came to serve.

This chapter invites and challenges you, the reader, to become aware of that which hinders you and your community of faith as it seeks to faithfully carry out its ministry of Christian education. Where are fear, false clarity, presumptions, routine, the tyranny of the urgent, denial of the messiness of life, and other hindrances that you might name present in your situation and affecting the work of renewing and transforming educational ministry?

It is hoped that in the naming of these hindrances, in coming to understand how they work in our lives, and in prayerfully confronting them we are empowered to move from fear to courage, from false clarity to openness, from presumptions to thoughtful attention, from routine to engaging diversity, from the tyranny of the urgent to radical patience, and from denial of the messiness of life to embracing complexity and ambiguity. If we engage in such movements, those things that hinder have the potential to become sources of insight, and our ministry will be blessed.

Reflection and Application

The following exercises are offered to assist readers in their engagement with the ideas presented in this chapter.

1. Name the hindrances you see at work in your church. Does your list include any of the ones discussed in this chapter? Which ones? What new ones do you name? Prioritize your list. Which hindrances are the strongest in your setting?

2. On a sheet of paper, list each hindrance you have named. Under each one, make a list of the ways in which you see that hindrance at work in your church. For example, is fear at work in people's avoidance of new ideas? Do you see the hindrance of routine at work in people's insistence that things be done the same way over and over again?

3. Make a list of presumptions related to Christian education that you believe are present in your church. Which of these presumptions are helpful? Which ones hinder you?

4. Strategize the steps your church could take to address the hindrances you have identified. How could you move from fear to courage, from false clarity to openness, and so on? Be specific.

5. What is the next step that you need to take to deal with the hindrances that are blocking the ministry of Christian education in your setting? Be specific about what it is, who will do it, and by when it will be done.

POSTSCRIPT

In a collection of wisdom tales, Noah BenShea tells of an encounter between a man named Jacob and a group of parents from the village in which he lives. Jacob, the village baker, is seen by some as a person of wisdom. Among those who find their way to his bakery to listen and talk with him are the children. Their parents are concerned about these gatherings and want to know what is going on. After all, he is just the baker, and what could he be teaching their children? In an encounter with a group of parents who come to confront him, Jacob says that he will be glad to tell them what he is teaching their children, but first he wants them to do something for him. He asks them to put their fingers in their ears. The parents do as they are told, and Jacob then begins speaking. After a few moments, the parents begin to wave their arms in frustration and call out to Jacob: "'Jacob...we can't hear what's being said when our fingers are in our ears!' 'That,' answered Jacob, 'is what I have been telling your children.'"[1]

The insight is obvious. We can't hear when our fingers are in our ears. We can't see when our hands cover our eyes. With the publication in 1990 of the Search Institute's report on the state of education in the church, we were invited to take our fingers out of our ears and our hands from in front of our eyes to see and hear some truth about this important ministry of the church. It has been several years since the research was conducted and the report was published, and it is my observation that we are still working to open our ears and eyes with regard to Christian education in the church today.

My hope is that the discussion presented in the preceding pages serves as a vehicle to assist those of us who care deeply about the educational ministry of the church to sharpen our hearing, clarify our seeing, and commit ourselves in renewed ways to carrying out the task of educating in faith. Effective Christian education occurs when all aspects of the church, including pastors, church educators, church governing bodies, laity, seminaries, and denominational staff, work together to think carefully and critically about the task of education and to provide strong support for the educational endeavors of the church.

Our challenge is to build for the future of the church. By laying the foundation proposed in this book, we will be putting in place the basic building blocks from which a strong and vital educational ministry can arise. The generations to come are dependent on our efforts. May we be faithful to our call!

FOR FURTHER READING

Methods

Crockett, Joseph V. *Teaching Scripture From An African-American Perspective*. Nashville: Discipleship Resources, 1990.

Furnish, Dorothy J. *Experiencing the Bible with Children*. Nashville: Abingdon Press, 1990.

Galindo, Israel. *The Craft of Christian Teaching*. Valley Forge, Penn.: Judson Press, 1998.

Griggs, Donald L. *Teaching Teachers To Teach*. Livermore, Calif.: Griggs Educational Service, 1974.

Halverson, Delia. *New Ways to Tell The Old, Old Story: Choosing and Using Bible Stories with Children and Youth*. Nashville: Abingdon Press, 1992.

LeFever, Marlene D. *Creative Teaching Methods*. Elgin, Ill.: David C. Cook, 1985.

Leypoldt, Martha M. *40 Ways to Teach in Groups*. Valley Forge, Penn.: Judson Press, 1967.

McCarthy, Bernice. *About Learning*. Barrington, Ill: Excel, 1996.

Osmer, Richard. *Teaching for Faith*. Louisville: Westminster John Knox Press, 1992.

Rusbuldt, Richard E. *Basic Teacher Skills*. Valley Forge, Penn: Judson Press, 1981.

Smith, Judy Gattis. *Joyful Teaching–Joyful Learning*. Nashville: Discipleship Resources, 1986.

———. *77 Ways to Energize Your Sunday School Class*. Nashville: Abingdon Press, 1992.

Van Ness, Patricia W. *Transforming Bible Study with Children*. Nashville: Abingdon Press, 1991.

Williams, Linda Verlee. *Teaching for the Two-sided Mind*. New York: Simon & Schuster, 1983.

Wimberly, Anne Streaty. *Soul Stories: African American Christian Education*. Nashville: Abingdon Press, 1994.

Wink, Walter. *Transforming Bible Study: A Leader's Guide.* Nashville: Abingdon Press, 1990.

Teaching in the Church

Caine, Renate Nummela, and Geoffrey Caine. *Making Connections: Teaching and the Human Brain.* Menlo Park, Calif: Addison-Wesley, 1994.

Foster, Charles R. *Teaching in the Community of Faith.* Nashville: Abingdon Press, 1982.

———. *The Ministry of the Volunteer Teacher.* Nashville: Abingdon Press, 1986.

Griggs, Donald L. *Planning for Teaching Church School.* Valley Forge, Penn.: Judson Press, 1985.

Halverson, Delia. *How Do Our Children Grow? Introducing Children to God, Jesus, the Bible, Prayer, Church.* Rev. ed. St. Louis: Chalice Press, 1999.

———. *How To Train Volunteer Teachers.* Nashville: Abingdon Press, 1991.

Jackson, Byron, ed. *Designs for Teacher Education.* Memphis: Board of Christian Education, Cumberland Presbyterian Church, 1982.

Joyce, Bruce, Marsha Weil, and Beverly Showers. *Models of Teaching.* 4th ed. Boston: Allyn and Bacon, 1992.

Little, Sara. *To Set One's Heart.* Atlanta: John Knox Press, 1983.

Palmer, Parker. *To Know As We Are Known.* San Francisco: Harper & Row, 1983.

NOTES

Introduction

[1]Peter L. Benson and Carolyn H. Eklin, *Effective Christian Education: A National Study of Protestant Congregations—A Summary Report on Faith, Loyalty, and Congregational Life* (Minneapolis: Search Institute, 1990). Two works that do a commendable job of examining and reflecting on the findings are Eugene C. Roehlkepartain, *The Teaching Church: Moving Christian Education to Center Stage* (Nashville: Abingdon Press, 1993) and David S. Schuller, ed. *Rethinking Christian Education* (St. Louis: Chalice Press, 1993).

[2]Benson and Eklin, 1.

[3]The denominations were the Christian Church (Disciples of Christ), the Evangelical Lutheran Church in America, the Presbyterian Church (USA), the United Church of Christ, The United Methodist Church, and the Southern Baptist Convention.

[4]Benson and Eklin, 3–4.

[5]Ibid., 58.

[6]Ibid., 42.

[7]Ibid., 58.

[8]Roehlkepartain, 20.

Chapter 1

Concept: What Is Christian Education?

[1]Charles F. Melchert, "Does the Church Really Want Religious Education?" *Religious Education* (Jan/Feb 1974):13–14.

[2]Thomas Groome, *Christian Religious Education* (San Francisco: Harper & Row, 1980), 20.

[3]In their book *Contemporary Approaches to Christian Education* (Nashville: Abingdon Press, 1982) Jack L. Seymour and Donald E. Miller offer descriptions of five approaches, or ways of naming educational ministry. I found some of their descriptive work to be helpful and have sought to incorporate some of their thinking here.

[4]Ibid., 36.

[5]Ibid., 53–71.

[6]See John Westerhoff, *Will Our Children Have Faith?* (New York: Seabury, 1983).

[7]Horace Bushnell, considered to be one of the forerunners of a socialization approach, understood conversion as a process occurring across time. His goal was for children to grow up as Christians and never know themselves to be otherwise. See *Christian Nurture* (New Haven, Conn.: Yale University Press, 1967).

[8]Seymour and Miller, 56.

[9]Ibid., 103.

[10]Daniel Aleshire, "Finding Eagles in the Turkeys' Nest: Pastoral Theology and Christian Education," *Review and Expositor* 85 (1988): 699.

[11]Ibid., 700.

[12]Ibid., 701–2.

[13]Groome, 25.

[14]Eugene C. Roehlkepartain, *The Teaching Church: Moving Christian Education to Center Stage* (Nashville:Abingdon Press, 1993), 87.

[15]Ibid.

[16]Maria Harris, *Fashion Me A People: Curriculum in the Chruch* (Louisville: Westminster/John Knox Press, 1989), 39.

[17]Ibid.

Chapter 2

Purpose: Why Do We Educate?

[1] *What's It All For? Reflections on the Purpose of Christian Education,* videocassette, prod. Estelle McCarthy and dir. Jeff Kellam, 30 min., Presbyterian School of Christian Education Video Education Center, 1988.

[2] Ibid.

[3] Daniel Aleshire, "Finding Eagles in the Turkeys' Nest: Pastoral Theology and Christian Education," *Review and Expositor* 85 (1988): 701–2.

[4] Thomas Groome, *Christian Religious Education* (San Francisco: Harper & Row, 1980), 34.

[5] Ibid., 35.

[6] Walter Brueggemann, *The Creative Word* (Philadelphia: Fortress Press, 1982), 1.

[7] Ibid.

[8] Ibid.

[9] Mary Elizabeth Moore, *Education for Continuity and Change* (Nashville: Abingdon Press, 1983), 14.

[10] Ibid., 18.

[11] Joseph A. Grassi, *Teaching the Way: Jesus, the Early Church and Today* (Lanham, Md.: University Press of America, 1982), 145.

[12] Moore, 22.

[13] Ibid., 120.

[14] Maria Harris, *Fashion Me A People: Curriculum in the Church* (Louisville: Westminster/John Knox Press, 1989), 23–24.

Chapter 3

Context: Where Do We Educate?

[1] Elliot W. Eisner, *The Educational Imagination,* 2d ed. (New York: Macmillan, 1985), 87–108.

[2] Ibid., 87.

[3] Ibid., 96.

[4] Maria Harris, *Fashion Me A People: Curriculum in the Church* (Louisville: Westminster/John Knox Press, 1989), 69.

[5] Eisner, 97.

[6] For further reading concerning the history of the Sunday school, see Robert W. Lynn and Elliott Wright, *The Big Little School: 200 Years of the Sunday School,* 2d ed., rev. (Birmingham, Ala.: Religious Education Press; Nashville: Abingdon Press,1980). Also Jack Seymour, "A Reforming Movement: The Story of the Protestant Sunday School," in *Renewing the Sunday School and the CCD,* ed. D. Campbell Wyckoff (Birmingham, Ala.: Religious Education Press, 1986).

[7] Seymour, 3.

[8] See Neil MacQueen, "Sunday School Is *Not* The Answer," *Church Educator* (February 1995): 5; and Wesley Taylor, "Growth Dynamics For Growing Church Schools," *Church Educator* (February 1995): 3–4, 13–14.

[9] D. Campbell Wyckoff, "As American As Crab Grass: The Protestant Sunday School," *Religious Education* 75, no. 1 (January–February 1980): 34.

[10] Seymour, 22.

[11] Robert W. Lynn, "A Historical Perspective on the Future of American Religious Education," in *Foundations of Christian Education in an Era of Change,* ed. Marvin Taylor (Nashville: Abingdon Press, 1976), 11.

[12] Eugene C. Roehlkepartain, *The Teaching Church: Moving Christian Education to Center Stage* (Nashville: Abingdon Press, 1993), 191.

[13] See Harris for a full discussion of these forms.

[14]I owe much of my thinking here to the work of Parker Palmer in *To Know As We Are Known* (San Francisco: Harper & Row, 1983).

[15]Ibid., 71.

[16]Ella P. Mitchell, "Oral Tradition: Legacy of Faith for the Black Church," *Religious Education* 81, no. 1 (Winter 1986): 93.

[17]Ibid., 95.

[18]Roehlkepartain, 167.

[19]Ibid., 171.

[20]Patricia Rice, "Program Here Gets Grant to Teach Tradition to Young Jewish Families," *St. Louis Post-Dispatch,* 13 January 1996, sec. D.

[21]See Peter Benson and Eugene Roehlkepartain, *Beyond Leaf Raking: Learning to Serve/Serving to Learn* (Nashville: Abingdon Press, 1993) for a thorough discussion of this concept and its use in the church.

[22]Benson and Roehlkepartain provide research and evidence for such a claim.

Chapter 4

Content: What Do We Need to Know?

[1]Maria Harris, *Fashion Me A People: Curriculum in the Church* (Louisville: Westminster/John Knox Press, 1989), 7.

[2]Ibid., 63.

[3]Karen Tye, "Those Who Teach: A Qualitative Investigation of How 'Church School Teacher' Is Described and Defined by Selected Local Presbyterian Church School Teachers" (Ed.D. diss., Presbyterian School of Christian Education, 1987), 82.

[4]See Anne Streaty Wimberly, *Soul Stories: African American Christian Education* (Nashville: Abingdon Press, 1994) for a full description of the story-linking approach. Susanne Johnson also discusses the importance of story and the different kinds of story to which we need to attend in her work *Christian Spiritual Formation in the Church and Classroom* (Nashville: Abingdon Press, 1989).

[5]Harris, 66.

[6]Eugene C. Roehlkepartain, *The Teaching Church: Moving Christian Education to Center Stage* (Nashville: Abingdon Press, 1993), 32.

[7]Thomas Groome, *Christian Religious Education* (San Francisco: Harper & Row, 1980), 25.

[8]Daniel Aleshire, "Finding Eagles in the Turkeys' Nest: Pastoral Theology and Christian Education" *Review and Expositor* 85 (1988): 699.

[9]Roehlkepartain, 120.

[10]See Thomas Greene, *The Activities of Teaching* (New York: McGraw-Hill, 1971) for an excellent discussion of the different ways of knowing. See also Groome's *Christian Religious Education,* especially chap. 7.

[11]Jane R. Martin, ed., *Readings in the Philosophy of Education: A Study of Curriculum* (Boston: Allyn and Bacon, 1970), 78.

[12]Groome, 142.

[13]Iris V. Cully, *Planning and Selecting Curriculum for Christian Education* (Valley Forge, Penn.: Judson Press, 1983), 24.

[14]Some of this material is adapted from Cully's work. See 111–13.

[15]Tye, 164.

Chapter 5

Participants: Whom Do We Educate?

[1]Daniel Aleshire, *Faithcare* (Philadelphia: Westminster Press, 1988), 9.

[2]See Nancy T. Foltz, ed., *Handbook of Adult Religious Education* (Birmingham, Ala.:

Religious Education Press, 1986), especially chap. 2, for a discussion of some of the biological issues related to adult education.

[3] Isabel Briggs Myers with Peter B. Myers, *Gifts Differing* (Palo Alto, Calif.: Davies-Black Publishing, 1995), xii. The particular approach to personality types explained in this book is a helpful perspective for understanding people and their psychological differences. Another resource that uses the Myers-Briggs approach and focuses specifically on issues related to teaching and learning is Gordon Lawrence, *People Types and Tiger Stripes*, 3d ed. (Gainesville, Fla: Center for Applications of Psychological Type, 1979).

[4] Ella P. Mitchell, "Oral Tradition: Legacy of Faith for the Black Church" *Religious Education* 81, no. 1 (Winter 1986): 73–112.

[5] Ibid., 111.

[6] To read more about these theories of development, I recommend the following: Jean Piaget and Barbel Inhelder, *The Psychology of the Child* (New York: Basic Books, 1969); Hans G. Furth, *Piaget for Teachers* (Englewood Cliffs, N.J.: Prentice-Hall, 1970); Erik Erikson, *Childhood and Society*, 2d ed. (New York: W. W. Norton, 1963); Erik Erikson, *Identity: Youth and Crisis* (New York: W. W. Norton, 1968); and James Fowler, *Stages of Faith* (San Francisco: Harper & Row, 1981). In addition to Fowler's work, the following provide helpful discussions of faith development theory: John Westerhoff, *Will Our Children Have Faith?* (New York: Seabury Press, 1983), and Kenneth Stokes, *Faith is a Verb* (Mystic, Conn.: Twenty-third Publications, 1989).

[7] The following works engage this topic in ways that are helpful for those working in education in the church and are particularly useful for discovering more about how people learn: Renate N. Caine and Geoffrey Caine, *Making Connections: Teaching and the Human Brain* (Menlo Park, Calif.: Addison-Wesley, 1994); Thomas Armstrong, *Multiple Intelligences in the Classroom* (Alexandria, Va: Association for Supervision and Curriculum Development, 1994); Linda Verlee Williams, *Teaching for the Two-Sided Mind* (New York: Touchstone, 1983); Robert Sylwester, *A Celebration of Neurons: An Educator's Guide to the Human Brain* (Alexandria, Va: Association for Supervision and Curriculum Development, 1995); and Bernice McCarthy, *About Learning* (Barrington, Ill.: Excel, 1996). See also Israel Galindo, *The Craft of Christian Teaching* (Valley Forge, Penn.: Judson Press, 1998), especially chaps. 3 and 4.

[8] Sylwester, 1. The information shared here about the brain is drawn from Sylwester's work.

[9] Caine and Caine, 13.

[10] Ibid., 91.

[11] See Caine and Caine, chap. 6, for an excellent discussion of this process.

[12] Marita Golden, *A Woman's Place* (Garden City, N.J.: Doubleday, 1986), 21.

[13] Waynne James and Michael Galbraith, "Perceptual learning styles: implications and techniques for the practitioner," *Lifelong Learning* (January 1985): 20–23.

[14] David Kolb, *Experiential Learning: Experience as the Source of Learning and Development* (Englewood Cliffs, N.J.: Prentice-Hall, 1984).

Chapter 6

Process and Method: How Do We Educate?

[1] See "For Further Reading" for a selected bibliography on methods.

[2] See "For Further Reading" for a selected bibliography of resources for working with teachers.

[3] Two particular approaches to education in the church that I would recommend to your attention are the shared Christian praxis approach developed by Thomas Groome and the storylinking process developed by Anne Streaty Wimberly. See Thomas Groome, *Christian Religious Education* (San Francisco: Harper & Row, 1980) and *Sharing Faith* (San Francisco: Harper SanFrancisco, 1991); and Anne Streaty Wimberly, *Soul Stories: African American Christian Education* (Nashville: Abingdon Press, 1994).

ᵉnate N. Caine and Geoffrey Caine, *Making Connections: Teaching and the Hu-ʔain* (Menlo Park, Calif.: Addison-Wesley, 1994), 113.

ʲJohn Dewey, *Experience and Education* (New York: Collier Books, 1938), 25.

⁶Caine and Caine, 5.

⁷Ibid., 6.

⁸Ibid., 113.

⁹Groome, *Sharing Faith.* See chap. 7.

¹⁰Groome, *Christian Religious Education*, 187.

¹¹Caine and Caine, 157.

¹²Groome, *Christian Religious Education*, 263.

¹³Michael E. Williams, "The Midwives' Story: An Image of the Faithful Friend," *Weavings* 7, no. 3 (May/June 1992): 18.

¹⁴Daniel Schipani, "Educating for Social Transformation" in *Mapping Christian Education*, ed. Jack Seymour (Nashville: Abingdon Press, 1997), 28.

¹⁵See William Myers, *Black and White Styles of Youth Ministry* (New York: Pilgrim Press, 1991).

¹⁶A particularly helpful list can be found in Israel Galindo's *The Craft of Christian Teaching* (Valley Forge, Penn.: Judson Press, 1998), app. B, 166–71.

¹⁷Maria Harris, *Women and Teaching* (New York: Paulist Press, 1988), 90.

Chapter 7

Assessment and Evaluation: How Are We Doing?

¹Several sources are available that provide helpful assessment suggestions and tools for use in the church. Among these are Eugene Roehlkepartain, *Exploring Christian Education Effectiveness: An Inventory for Congregational Leaders* (Minneapolis: Search Institute, 1990); idem, *The Teaching Church: Moving Christian Education to Center Stage* (Nashville: Abingdon Press, 1993); and Jackson W. Carroll, Carl S. Dudley, and William McKinney, eds., *Handbook for Congregational Studies* (Nashville: Abingdon Press, 1986).

²Charles Foster points out the importance of opportunities for informal conversation for the educational ministry of the church in his chapter "Communicating: Informal Conversation in the Congregation's Education," in *Congregations: Their Power to Form and Transform*, ed. C. Ellis Nelson (Atlanta: John Knox Press, 1988), 218–37. Margaret Ann Crain also highlights the value of dialogue and listening to people in her chapter "Listening to Churches: Christian Education in Congregational Life," in *Mapping Christian Education*, ed. Jack L. Seymour (Nashville: Abingdon Press, 1997), 93–109.

³Elliot W. Eisner, *The Enlightened Eye: Qualitative Inquiry and the Enhancement of Educational Practice* (New York: Macmillan, 1991), 1.

⁴Peter L. Benson and Carolyn H. Eklin, *Effective Christian Education: A National Study of Protestant Congregations—A Summary Report on Faith, Loyalty, and Congregational Life* (Minneapolis: Search Institute, 1990), 9.

⁵Thomas Groome, *Christian Religious Education* (San Francisco: Harper & Row, 1980), 34.

Chapter 8

Hindrances: What Stands in Our Way?

¹Carlos Castañeda, *The Teachings of Don Juan: A Yaqui Way of Knowledge* (New York: Pocket Books, 1968), 82.

²Henri Nouwen, *Lifesigns* (Garden City, N.J.: Doubleday, 1986), 15–16.

³Castañeda, 85.

⁴Paulo Freire, *Pedagogy of the Oppressed* (New York: Sea

⁵Rainer Maria Rilke, *Letters to a Young Poet* (New York:)

⁶Karen Tye, "Those Who Teach: A Qualitative Investiga
School Teacher' Is Described and Defined by Selected Local H
School Teachers" (Ed.D. diss., Presbyterian School of Christian Edu

⁷Daniel Aleshire, *Faithcare* (Philadelphia: Westminster Press, 198

⁸Ibid., 23.

⁹Ibid., 17.

¹⁰Ibid., 35.

¹¹Sue Bender, *Plain and Simple* (San Francisco: HarperCollins, 1989), 14ь

Postscript

¹Noah BenShea, *Jacob the Baker: Gentle Wisdom for a Complicated World* (New York: Ballantine Books, 1989), 65–68.